S0-AIT-318

AIRBORNE
ALBUM

1943-1945
NORMANDY TO VICTORY

By John Andrews

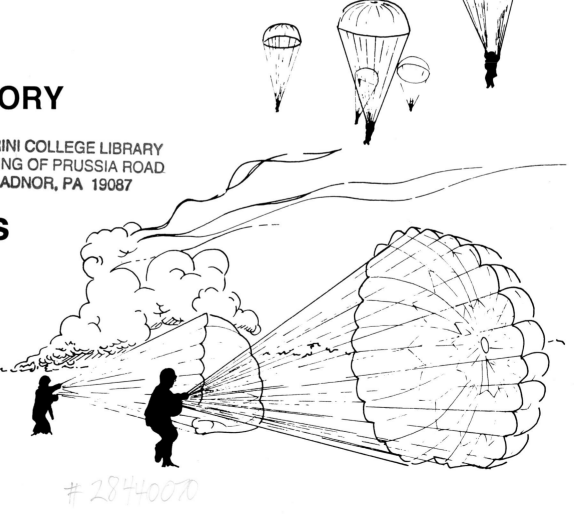

Phillips
Publications

Sightseeing in Exotic New Guinea: Jungle Dogface PFC Emery Graham of the 503rd's regimental headquarters company. His burden includes a rolled up hammock/mosquito bar, musette bag with dangling steel pot and machete (from its mottled grip, probably an Australian-contract item) tucked under its flap. One-piece coveralls were generally disliked, because they made answering calls of nature very awkward. (Emery Graham)

PHILLIPS PUBLICATIONS, INC.
P.O. Box 168, Williamstown, N.J. 08094-0168
609-567-0695
L.C.C. 81-82475
I.S.B.N. 0-93257-07-3

**IN MEMORIAM
DUFFIELD WALKER MATSON
10 June 1924-28 October 1989**

While this book is dedicated to all the valiant soldiers who built the reputation of the American Airborne with blood, sweat and tears, we are compelled to recognize one in particular: Duff Matson. Born in the Shenandoah country of Virginia and raised in Florida, Duff was by his own admission a "wild, out-of-control kid" who thought he had found his calling as a hell-bent cutthroat in the Airborne. It took the shock of a 30-year sentence to Leavenworth and the fortuitous intervention of General Frederick to change the course of his life. Finishing the war with distinction, he returned home to win acclaim in the community and fortune in the business world. We miss this soft-spoken giant among men and ask God's mercy for him.

THE BEGINNINGS

The first American to envision air-landed troops
[i]s Benjamin Franklin, inspired by the sight of hot-
[air] balloons in France in 1784. In 1918, airpower
[pr]ophet Billy Mitchell hatched a plan for the vertical
[en]velopment of the German fortress at Metz in early
[19]19; the scheme faded away with the Armistice.

It was not until April 1939 that the U.S. Army
[loo]ked into "Air Infantry" as a tool for the mobile
[de]fense of Panama, Alaska, and the Philippines.
[Th]is quest discovered the sizable German, Soviet,
[Ita]lian and French efforts. In early 1940, the project
[wa]s given to a bright and diligent staff officer, Major
[Wi]lliam C. Lee. Lee was to become "The Father
[of] the American Airborne." Working with the Infan-
[try] Board at Fort Benning, he gave up on the idea
[of] air-landing troops in transport aircraft against lit-
[tle] or no opposition and instead worked to use para-
[ch]utes and gliders to insert units under fire.

[L]ee and Benning worked to bring together the
[Air] Corps and the Infantry. By small steps, opera-
[tio]nal theories and materiel were tested. Once speci-
[me]ns of the new T-4 troop parachute — meant to
[ca]rry a fully-equipped infantryman, unlike smaller-
[ca]nopy "aircrew escape" types — were in hand,
[or]ders were passed to the Infantry School's "demon-
[str]ation unit," the 29th Infantry Regiment, to detach
[me]n for temporary duty in a Parachute Test Platoon.

[O]n 26 June 1940, a call for one lieutenant and
[48] enlisted men was made. Even with stiff criteria,
[ap]plicants numbered 17 and over 200, respectively.

Rigorous screening reduced the field to 49 men, with the overage justified
as a hedge against expected casualties. Through July and into August, the
PTP underwent intense physical training and combat skills classes — and
waited for chutes and aircraft. The Platoon visited the Safe Parachute Company in Hightstown, New Jersey, to ride the 250-foot jump towers that had
been amusements at the 1939 New York World's Fair.

Actual jumps began on 16 August 1940. It took three days of C-39's (mi-
liarized Douglas DC-2's) flying "racetracks" at 1,500 feet over Lawson Field
to complete two "tap-out" jumps per soldier. "Mass" jumps of "sticks" of
about 10 parachutists were conducted at 750 feet in the days following. On
29 August, General Marshall was a spectator for the fifth and final descent.
In his remarks, he announced that Parachute Battalions had been authorized and would soon begin activation.

[On] 29 August 1940, the Parachute Test Platoon made
[its] fifth and final jump, ending the experiment that
[pro]ved the feasibility of parachute troops. For that oc-
[ca]sion, the sun-helmeted Maj. Gen. George A. Lynch
[(W]ar Department Chief of Infantry) and Maj. William
[C.]Lee (his Airborne project officer) had their picture
[tak]en with Lt. William T. Ryder (right rear) and a
["st]ick" of PTP soldiers (left to right): Pvt. Richard J.
[Ke]lly, PFC Mitchel Guilbeau, Pvt. William N. "Red"
[Kin]g, Pvt. Ernest L. Dilburn, PFC Alsie L. Rutland, and
[Pvt]. Joseph E. Doucet. (101st Airborne Division As-
[so]ciation)

1

Medics of the 504th Parachute Battalion, 1941.

In late November 1940 Ed Smith returned from the first class for parachute riggers at Chanute Field, Illinois, and spent some of his pay on this portrait, a Christmas gift for his parents. The odd rockers below his PFC chevron are non-regulation, ''for optional wear'' and stand for the top within-rank Rating of Specialist First Class. Such ratings were common among Air Corps technicians, cooks, and bandsmen from the 1920's to the middle of 1942, when they were supplanted by the Technician series. They conferred extra pay, but no NCO status. For the 501st Parachute Battalion, they were granted in the days between the loss of flight pay (effective with the end of the PTP) and the creation of Parachute Pay (May 1941). The $54 per month salary of the ''First and First'' grade was on a par with that of some 1st Sergeants in ''normal'' outfits. Note that the parachute cap disc is the only insignia of a paratrooper at this time, as jump wings were not awarded until the following March. (Edward R. Smith)

s group is probably from the 501st Parachute Battalion, in mid-1941. Minus Air Corps officer at center, they wear the ''balloon cloth'' jump suit and aircrew toque helmet. Note that their boots lack the ankle strap.

Carolina Maneuvers. October-November 1941: On the basis of the leftmost man being tentatively identified as Robert Bertie, this group may be from the 502nd Parachute Battalion. The horsehide bibs attached to the Riddell helmets were to fend off pine boughs.

Panama, 501st Parachute Battalion, 1941-1942: Elmer W. Noll and L. Kurtz model the ''M1941'' jump suit. Their parachute cap discs may be the oversized style otherwise associated with The Parachute School cadremen. (Elmer Noll)

Experimental jump suits: the shiny ''balloon-cloth'' Suit, Parachute Jumper with new pockets; and two cotton twill antecedents of the M1941. (Information courtesy of Shelby L. Stanton)

3

The "M1941 jump suit" (suit, parachute jumper) modeled in the Washingto[n] offices of the Quartermaster General. This precursor of the famous "M194[2] jump outfit was issued only briefly, but showed up later in Panama and Nor[th] Africa. (U.S. Army)

The Airborne Force Grows

On 6 September 1940, the "1st Parachute Battalion" was constitute[d] Ten days later this designation was amended to "501st," partly to differe[n]tiate it from the Marine Corps' 1st Parachute Battalion also then formin[g] Between late 1940 and late 1941, the Army Airborne grew through the a[c]tivation of four Parachute battalions, the Parachute School, and their high[est] headquarters, the Provisional Parachute Group.

It was also in this period that the Glider arm began to take shape. Co[m]pelled by the Luftwaffe's 1940 success in Belgium, the Air Corps got t[he] biplane-maker Waco to design the 15-place CG-4, with the first of them [de]livered on 14 May 1941. The dramatic seizure of Crete by the Germans [in] that same month soon expanded plans for the glider program, but inept ma[n]agement delayed delivery of both the aircraft and the men to fly them [for] many months. Other than a token force of 19 Wacos that carried British a[s]sets in the invasion of Sicily, there were no American gliders in combat u[ntil] 1944.

With the advent of real war, the Pentagon abandoned "Hemispheric D[e]fense" in favor of the offense, with strong expeditionary forces bringing t[he] war to the Axis. Among the changes resulting from this new Big Pictu[re] Parachute Infantry Regiments were formed. During the spring of 1942, t[he] four existing Battalions became the basis for three new PIR's, all of the[m] then separate units.

The next stage in expansion saw Airborne Divisions created. Two we[re] established, effective 15 August 1942. The already-active 82nd Motoriz[ed] Division was reshuffled with newly-embodied elements of the paper-Reser[ve] 101st Infantry Division to give birth to Airborne Divisions — each two-thir[ds] Glider and one-third Parachute — bearing the same numbers.

Even though just a third of each Airborne Division's personnel were [ex]pected to be paratroopers, it proved a Herculean task to train them (a[nd] the separate units). It was not just prying loose thousands of volunteers fr[om] training centers and putting them to work jumping. In 1942, everything b[ut] confusion was in short supply, especially parachutes and C-47's and g[lid]ers. The 11th Airborne Division — the first formed from scratch and reli[ant] on draftees — could not be activated until February 1943.

The Cattaraugus 225Q and Case 337Q knives were pre-existing models of civilian hunting knives purchased by the Quartermaster Corps (whence the "Q") in 1942 to supplement stocks of the World War I trench knife. Though used during the North African and New Guinea campaigns, they fell into disuse when the M-3 became available.

rocco, June 1943. Details of the C-47 troop carrier's "parapack" racks are own here, as mortarmen of the 505th PIR load up for a training drop. Their ain chutes are rigged with free-fall rip-cords. (U.S. Army)

..is Air Corps photo purports to show actual embarkation for the Sicily jump, t the free-fall parachutes (possibly the B-7 type with QAC reserve) and gas asks suggest otherwise. (U.S. Air Force)

Lawson Field, 1941: Jump school instructor Donald O. Graul makes do with the obsolescent blue denim dungaree "fatigues." Graul was later commissioned, assigned as the communications platoon leader of the 507th PIR, and captured in Normandy. (Charles T. Graul)

5

Into the Fiery Abyss: Baptism in Afric[a]

A day-time sentry in Trapani checks the driver of an RAF truck. The mafia was strong there, and the 82nd Airborne undertook a "combat mission" to make it clear that wholesale theft of government stores, rampant crime and attacks on its men would not be tolerated.

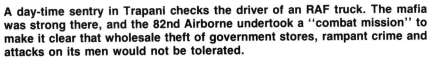

After a hard-fought battle defending the critical terrain of the Biazzo Ridge against elements of the Luftwaffe's Hermann Goring Panzer Division, the commander of the 3rd Battalion, 505th Parachute Infantry, Lt. Col. Edward C. Krause, and an unidentified paratrooper take possession of a bit of booty — a 75mm PAK 40 anti-tank gun. The enlisted man wears a Luftwaffe belt and bayonet set, another freshly-acquired souvenir. (U.S. Army)

It was not a Parachute Infantry Regiment, let alone an Airborne Divisio[n] that first served in battle or made combat jumps. It was an "orphan" B[at]talion, that was fated to make five combat jumps but go largely unnotic[ed]. Its lineage was peculiar: born as the 504th Parachute Battalion, it was th[en] merged into the 503rd PIR as its 2nd Battalion. Soon thereafter, it was [de]tached from its new parent and sent to England in June 1942. From the[re] it jumped into Algeria, as part of the TORCH invasion, on 8 November 19[42]. It made two more combat jumps in North Africa and distinguished itsel[f in] battles along the Tunisian frontier, months before the 82nd Airborne D[ivi]sion arrived. (Meanwhile, the rest of the 503rd PIR was sent to Austra[lia.] To tidy up loose ends, the errant battalion became "2/509th PIR." Lat[er,] with no other parts of this Regiment activated, it was redesignated as a se[pa]rate Battalion.)

The 509th prided itself on being the true pioneers of paratrooping and [did] not get along well with the hierarchy of the 82nd Airborne Division, to wh[ich] it was attached May-September 1943. Bored with training in Morocco, ma[ny] 509ers volunteered for TDY as air gunners on B-25's. Not quite good enou[gh] for the 82nd, the OSS and Airborne Training Center staff eagerly recruited the[m].

Ever the stepchild, the 509th was relegated to reserve for HUSKY. Ev[en] when the 504th lost hundreds of men to "friendly" fire and the 82nd inheri[ted] a protracted ground campaign, they were not called forward. When the 82[nd] planned to drop on Rome, the provisional Scout Company got the job of qua[sh]ing the pesky German radar on the isle of Ventotene. The main miss[ion] scrubbed, nobody passed the word to the scouts, who kept going. The "[sui]cide mission" at Avellino was a concept that had come up in earlier plans[,] but in daylight and using at least one PIR. A citation and several individ[ual] awards for Avellino seemed to be deliberately "lost" passing through Ridgwa[y's] HQ.

Such perceived insults did not heal quickly. After the main body of the 82nd headed for England, the 509th got along famously with the 504th RCT, shar[ing] the adversities of slogging through the winter around Venafro. Anzio fo[und] both jump outfits attached to the 3rd Infantry Division — another vacation w[ith] cold mud and hot steel.

A pair of troopers from the ever-independent 509th PIR relax after the first U.S. combat jumps. PFC Jack Monreal drives his Harley Davidson, November 1942. (Yarborough)

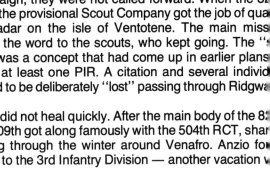

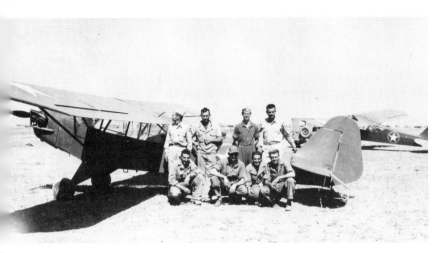

Personnel of the Flight Section, Headquarters and Headquarters Battery, 82nd Division Artillery and a Piper L-4 "Cub" spotter plane at Trapani, Sicily. (82nd Airborne Division Museum)

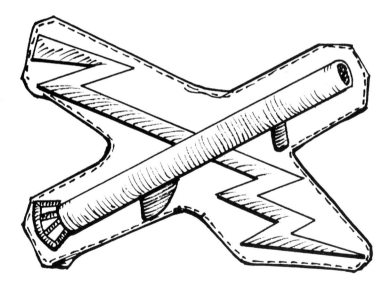

James Gavin, then a Colonel commanding the 505th PIR, created this badge to recognize bazookamen. A few dozen were embroidered by Sicilian nuns in exchange for rations and medical care (they weren't interested in cigarettes); the bazooka and lightning flash were blue and red.

The Pause That Refreshes: This trio of 505 troopers has discovered gelato, Sicilian-style ice cream. The man on the left is marked as a probable bazookaman by his goggles and what appears to be the special "Tank-Killer" patch on his sleeve. A first aid packet hangs from the bottom of his trouser pocket. The center figure has a liberated pistol on his jacket belt. The soldier on the right is a medic, with his distinctive bag bearing a Red Cross brassard. He wears a camouflage parachute silk scarf and the issue pouch for the lensatic compass. (U.S. Air Force)

Canadians of the 1st Special Service Force enjoy an ice cream treat in the dusty cantonment at Fort William Henry Harrison, Montana. Their British-style "sidecap" headgear marks them as non-US troops. The A-2 horsehide flight jacket, from the Air Corps supply system, was general issue in the Force; one man has jump wings painted on his. (1st Special Service Force Association)

The "Red Devils" of the 508th PIR dubbed this activity "Muscle College": injury-defying calisthenics performed with treetrunks, going beyond individual exercise to instill timing and teamwork. Only after squads proved nimble were they trusted to cooperate in a platoon performance as shown here. (17th Airborne Division Association)

This shot shows how American chutes deployed: The Static Line (with its other end connected by a Snap Hook to the Anchor Cable inside the plane) is attached to the webbing of the Cover Panel Assembly at its center and tied with cord to the Apex of the Canopy; when the line is played out to its maximum (as here), a first tug breaks the cord lacing the panel to the Parachute Pack; when the Shroud Lines are pulled taut and the canopy is filled with air, the Opening Shock will break the tie at the apex. The lines and panels will stay with the aircraft, hanging in the slipstream until the jumpers are gone and the aircrew or jumpmaster hauls them. (John C. Grady)

photographic evidence of the Marine Corps glider program: the fifth of 13 Schweizer LNS-1 (Army TG-2) trainers, at Cherry Point. (National Archives)

Parachute Marines in action on Bougainville, November 1943. Three carry M-1A1 folding-stock carbines — a type not found on the unit's table of authorized equipment. The other has a Springfield with rubber butt cup, the mark of a rifle grenadier's weapon. Perhaps all their camouflaged jump smocks, made as step-ins, have been altered by cutting off the closed crotches and turning up the hems under the pockets, making a full-fly jacket. (U.S. Marine Corps)

Marine jump boots were patterned after the Corps' standard "boondocker" rough-out field shoes. Privately acquired Corcoran-type boots were also worn, especially by men of the California-based 2nd and 4th Battalions, bloused Army fashion with Class A and B uniforms.

The USMC adopted at least three models of step-in jump smocks, in solid green HBT cloth and camouflage fabric. This type — recognizable by its diagonal snap-closure chest pockets — was worn in combat.

9

Irony in the jungle: Maj. Harry L. Torgerson, 1st Marine Parachute Battalion, savors his yuletide necktie and a cigar, just arrived from home, November 1943. His weapon is a "Type R carbine" that combines features of the rifle and machine gun Johnsons. Only a handful of these were made, and Torgerson was given his by the inventor himself. (U.S. Marine Corps).

This group on Bougainville is a mixture of "Paramarines" and Raiders. M are identifiable as the former by their jump boots. The Marine with a fold carbine has a non-issue Smith & Wesson revolver poking out of his ch pocket. The figure at right in plain green utilities totes a New Zealand-m knuckle-knife and, lacking a firearm, may be a Navy Corpsman.

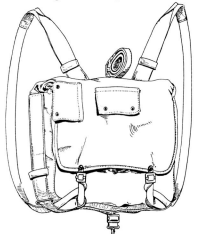

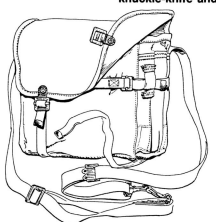

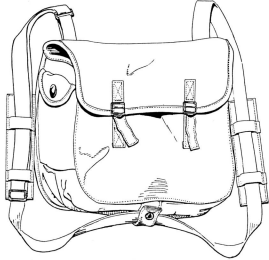

USMC radio bag.

The Marine Corps used several items of load-bearing equipment (vernacularly "782 gear," after its supply code) that did not follow Army designs, among them a two-part pack system. This is the haversack, the all-purpose upper unit with integral suspenders and rolled-up top strap for the shelter half and/or poncho. To augment this, the "knapsack" lower unit was added below.

Like the Army, the Marine Corps had a Field Bag or "Musette" in the m meant for officers, and like the Army Airborne the Marine parachute u adapted it for more general use. The USMC pattern differs in details.

Jump-booted SSgt. Spearman of HHC, 325th Glider Infantry Regiment's communications platoon tries to operate during Exercise TIGER, near Slapton Sands, England, late April 1944. Radioman Pvt. Battenberg wears the more usual shoes and leggings of a gliderman. (82nd Airborne Division Museum)

The "walkie-talkie" radio was officially the Radio Set SCR-536. Minus strap and batteries, its major part was the Radio Receiver and Transmitter BC-611. A technological innovation with a theoretical range of perhaps two miles, it was not popular with paratroops because of its fragility and unreliability — before Normandy, the 507th PIR decided they would just holler a lot, and not bother with them.

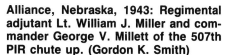

Alliance, Nebraska, 1943: Regimental adjutant Lt. William J. Miller and commander George V. Millett of the 507th PIR chute up. (Gordon K. Smith)

To prove to the folks back home that he was really a paratrooper, eighteen-year-old Lee Hulett had this photo taken while assigned to the Demolition Platoon, HHC, 517th PIR of the 17th Airborne Division (Lee S. Hulett).

The quintessential Glider Artilleryman: Cpl. Carl Leydig, Battery A. 680th GFAB, Camp Forrest, Tennessee. Leydig was among the first crop of Glidermen sent to Divisional jump school for cross-qualification — when a colonel from headquarters visited the training and discovered they were NOT volunteers, he proclaimed anyone who wanted was welcome to leave, and Leydig was the "first one out the door." He wasn't much scared — gliders were plenty scary — but he believed in the First Rule of Soldiering: Never Volunteer. (Carl Leydig)

The G-2 Section of the 17th Airborne Division headquarters staff, as it looked during the Tennessee maneuvers in November 1943. Front row, left to right: Raymond Just, Richard Lacefield, Fred O. Dickson, George Charlesworth. Middle row: Thomas Conners, Hans Kessler, Adolf Beyers, Glen Miller, Raymond Fenton. Back row: Lt. Col. Kent, Maj. Lyle McAlister. (Richard Lacefield)

Redlegs of the 466th Parachute Field Artillery Battalion, 17th Airborne Division, ready for the field at Camp Mackail, early 1944. (Left to right): Symczak, Alvarez, unidentified, Legeditch (kneeling), Hawkins, two unidentified, and Pietrowicz (17th Airborne Division Assoc.).

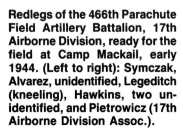

Gun crew of Battery A, 460th PFAB in wintry Tennessee: Sgt. Kearny, Bartinski, Leroy Herdman, I.J. Bart, Roger Tallakson. (Roger Tallakson).

A member of A-680th stands in the driving sleet of Tennessee to show off the "invisibility" of his get-up. The camouflage coveralls did not do as well in pine groves as they might in the jungle, and the red band on the helmet (to mark opposing sides in war games) did not help. (Carl Leydig)

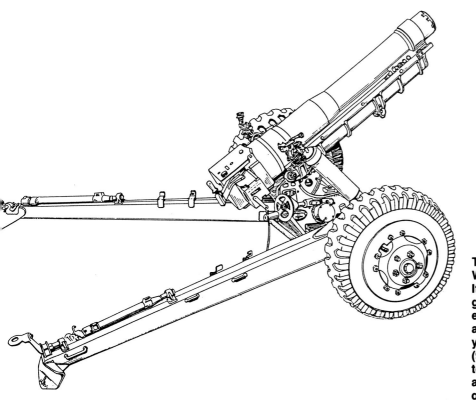

Though obscure, the M-3 105mm pack howitzer was widely issued during World War II to the Cannon Companies organic to non-Airborne Infantry Regiments. It was developed (using many components from the full-size One-O-Five) to give Glider Field Artillery a weapon heavier than the pack 75. But it could not easily use standard 105mm ammo (supplied with five to seven powder charges) and its special ammo was a logistic annoyance. Its maximum range of 7,600 yards (later stretched to 8,400) was actually less than that of the smaller piece (9,600 yards). As a result, the one GFAB per Airborne Division designated to use it often chose to replace it with the 75. It was, however, much used at Bastogne, where seven-charge rounds made firing tables meaningless and quickly wore it out.

13

OVERLORD: The Legend Grows

The most famous mission in the annals of the U.S. Airborne — Operation OVERLORD, the invasion of Normandy — began when 20 planes carrying Pathfinders lifted off, at 2150 hours on 5 June 1944. At 16 minutes after midnight the first of the "First In" trailblazers (from the 502nd PIR) hit the silk. Mere minutes later the teams of other regiments of both the 101st and 82nd Airborne Divisions went out the door to climax months of careful preparation and tedious rehearsal.

But the best-laid plans of mere mortals oft' go awry, and the ensuing misadventures of the Pathfinders set the tone for the whole drop. After the smooth fast-and-low run-in over the Contentin peninsula from the west, unexpected ground fog and a strip of cloud masked the last checkpoints from the view of the troop carrier crews. Then German flak awoke to maul eight of the transports. Though disoriented and distracted, the keyed-up aviators gave the "Go!" command and the torchbearers went. By then most of the C-47's were flying too high and/or too fast. Many sticks hit the icy blast at between 1,000 and 2,000 feet altitude and 100 knots speed. Punished by nasty chute problems and subjected to sporadic enemy fire on the long, long ride down, the Pathfinder teams were disrupted before they even came to earth.

OVERLORD dry-run, Upottery airfield, 4 June 1944: Soldiers of Company D, 325 GIR make the acquaintance of their glider for the D + 1 follow-up landings. No the hasty painting-over of the Horsa's RAF roundel with the American star-an bar emblem, minus all but one smear of white. This load of 29 riflemen was fat to have a fairly good landing, as the after-action report shows Horsa W-36 damaged, but with no injuries, and a mere 1,500 yards off the LZ. (U.S. Air Forc

This shot of 507th PIR officers dates from late May 1944. Front: Lt. Col. Edwin Ostberg, commander of the 1st Battalion (wounded in Normandy); Maj. Joseph Fagan; Lt. Col. Arthur Maloney, regimental executive officer (wounded); Lt. Col. Charles Timmes, commander of 2nd Battalion; Lt. Col. William Kuhn, commander of 3rd Battalion; Capt. (Chaplain) Robert Hennon (killed); Capt. (Chaplain) John Verret (captured); Maj. Gordon Smith, S-4 (wounded and captured); Maj. Ben Pearson, S-3 (wounded); Maj. George Vollmar, surgeon; Capt. James Dickerson, S-2 (killed in VARSITY); Maj. Charles Johnson, XO of 1st Battalion (killed in The Bulge). (Gordon K. Smith)

The most accurate Pathfinder drop in the 101st's objective area put tv of the three teams belonging to the 506th Parachute Infantry Regiment with walking distance of (but not on) Drop Zone "C" adjoining Hiesville. On t other hand, the 506th's third stick was put out over the English Channel (wit out fatalities). In the 82nd's bailiwick, only the Pathfinders of the 505th P hit their mark, DZ "O" near St. Mere-Eglise. Unlike all the other units jum ing in OVERLORD, the Five-O-Five had experience in both combat jum and ground combat. Moreover, the concept of specialized Pathfinders (fir dreamed of by the British Airborne, then Americanized by the independe 509th Parachute Infantry Battalion) had been nurtured by its previous cor mander, "Slim Jim" Gavin, recently promoted to Assistant Division Co mander.

Because of their dispersion, in many cases Pathfinder teams did not kno where they were in relation to their intended locations. Rather than add the confusion, some teams did not switch on their EUREKA radar beacol and mutely stood by while the main lift passed above. But other teams who variously did or did not realize the problem — did turn on. Hence, fe Pathfinders had a traceable, positive effect on the mass drops. The conf sion mounted as enemy fire, poor visibility, and aircrews' inexperience cor bined. No matter all the plans. For the real thing, Chaos reigned.

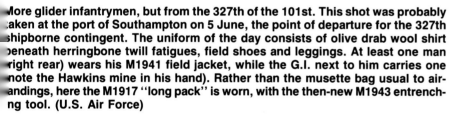

More glider infantrymen, but from the 327th of the 101st. This shot was probably taken at the port of Southampton on 5 June, the point of departure for the 327th shipborne contingent. The uniform of the day consists of olive drab wool shirt beneath herringbone twill fatigues, field shoes and leggings. At least one man (right rear) wears his M1941 field jacket, while the G.I. next to him carries one (note the Hawkins mine in his hand). Rather than the musette bag usual to air-landings, here the M1917 "long pack" is worn, with the then-new M1943 entrenching tool. (U.S. Air Force)

The FIRST stick into Normandy: Lt. Frank L. Lillyman's team poses with Aircraft –1 at North Witham on 5 June 1944. Out the door at 0016 hours the next morning, this group missed DZ A by a mile and set up near St. Germain-de-Varreville. Only partly because of that mishap, nary a stick of their 502nd and 377th PFAB "customers" hit the DZ. They were mainly spread in a swath north of the objective or let loose over DZ C when pilots saw blazing fires and lots of chutes on the ground. The use of pouches for Thompson magazines strung horizontally on pack suspenders is bizarre. (Dave Berry)

With little reliable ground guidance, the main drops were widely scattered. Jump mishaps and German counteraction aside, paratroopers who were convinced they had memorized every nuance of Normandy topography found themselves lost and bewildered. The natives' quaint hedgerows and cowpaths made a damned labyrinth. The Nazis' flooding made things a lot damper than foreseen and put bodies of water on the ground where they weren't on the map. It proved a remarkable event when more than three planeloads (about 40 men) from the same battalion could assemble in the darkness. If they could find the cargo bundles that in theory had left the plane with them, jubilation was in order.

But dispersion proved something of a two-edged sword: 13,000 very angry paratroopers were emerging from the murk, set on killing a lot of Germans in a short space of time. If the All-Americans and Screaming Eagles were frustrated in adhering to the master plan, the defenders had no real plan. The reality of ghostly wild Indians on the warpath did not much resemble the neat airheads the defenders had been primed to deal with. The dogs of war

let loose, the foe was demoralized by unpredictable attacks and persuaded that he was "cut off by superior forces." While the plans were crystal-clear to the generals on both sides, they were of no import at all on the platoon level.

The initial airborne assault phase of the Normandy battle boiled down from the level of the Division to that of the battalion. With whatever packets of miscellaneous troopers that passed within reach, and generally bereft of radio contact, 18 paratrooper battalion commanders set to work to complete their missions. In the large sense, the Airborne's purpose was to assist the escape of seaborne forces from a box-within-a-box. If Field Marshal Rommel was to be denied the chance to destroy the invaders on the beaches, the inner box would have to be breached by capturing the causeways that crossed the coastal marshes. To smash the outer box, the bridges that spanned the Merderet and Douve Rivers had to be seized. In demolishing these boxes the bloody but unbowed parachute infantrymen wrote their chapter in the legend of the Airborne.

Pathfinder Team, Aircraft Chalk Number 15, 1st Battalion, 507th PIR, D-1. A ba[s]ic Pathfinder team consisted of a lieutenant and nine enlisted men. Rather th[an] waste the several additional spaces in the C-47, many teams were augment[ed] with extra Pathfinders or men from HQ, engineer, medical, or other units. L[eft] to right, front: William O. Armstrong, Thomas E. Munden, Vincent Brophy, Jo[hn] Despot (with medical bag), Zigmund Hojnowski, Chalmer D. Hansen, Paul [E.] Pachowka, Fred L. Burns, John C. Mortzfeldt (an add-on volunteer from A/504[th]), 1LT Charles R. O'Brien, Jr. Rear: William R. Wolf, Robert Mitchell, two unide[n]tified, Jones H. Warren, unidentified, Robert E. Olsen, J. Morris Thompson, Jo[hn] R. Bergendahl. Not in picture: team leader 1LT Quinton P. Sunday. (John Desp[ot])

The harnesses of the T-5 Modified with the British Quick Release and T-5.

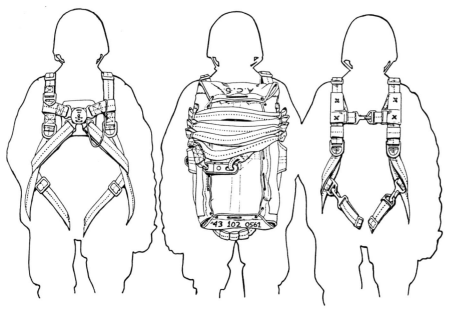

The night of 4/5 June found the Airborne ready to board their planes, but [a] "weather hold" delayed events until Ike decided to make a go of it. Here C[ol.] Robert L. Sink, commanding the 506th (Five-O-Sink) PIR confers with his A[ir] Forces counterpart, 439th Troop Carrier Group leader Col. Charles H. Youn[g]. (Col. Charles Young via 101st Airborne Division Association).

The commander of 3/506th PIR, Lt. Col. Robert S. Wolverton, helps Capt. Stanley E. Morgan prior to takeoff from Exeter. Wolverton died as he set foot to French soil, in a DZ trap set up by the enemy. While noting the helmet markings, observe that the tick-mark is on the wrong side for the 3rd Battalion! (U.S. Air Force)

Bazookaman Dick Knudsen of the 506th uses no helmet marking at all. In addition to a full-length M-1 rocket launcher halfway inside a British "B Bag," he has put his carbine in a heavy leather scabbard meant for military policemen on motorcycles. The jumper behind him has a M-3 "Grease Gun" slung below his chest chute. (U.S. Air Force)

This 506 trooper is not identified, but may be Lt. Col. Wolverton, leader of the 3rd Battalion. (U.S. Army)

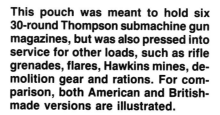

This pouch was meant to hold six 30-round Thompson submachine gun magazines, but was also pressed into service for other loads, such as rifle grenades, flares, Hawkins mines, demolition gear and rations. For comparison, both American and British-made versions are illustrated.

"Cricket," "audible recognition signals" were issued to most parachutists for OVERLORD. They came in several types, including insects (upper), frogs, cartoon characters, and austere brass styles (lower), all procured from the civilian toy market in the United Kingdom.

17

Soldiers of the 502nd PIR mind some surviving Krauts.

The 82nd Airborne Division led by Maj. Gen. Matthew B. Ridgway — li[k]
all units landing on D-Day — was overstrength. It had under its commar
three Parachute Infantry Regiments (PIR), each of three battalions. Thes
were the 505th "Panthers," the 507th "Spiders," and the 508th "Red Devils
The 507th and 508th had come to Britain under the command of the 2nd A[i]
borne Brigade and (like the Brigade staff) were attached, rather than pe[r]
manently assigned. Even the 505th had not been originally part of th[e]
All-American. It joined the Division just before it had shipped overseas, r[e]
inforcing the 504th PIR. The 504th was not participating in OVERLORD [as]
a unit, as it had only recently been reunited with the 82nd after a harrowin[g]
winter of detached service in Italy.

In Col. William Ekman's 505th, the 1st Battalion was to take the villag[e]
of La Fiere, where a road atop a causeway spanned the flooded Merder[et]
Its men were badly scattered on both sides of the river. But elements of th[e]
1/505, and more troopers belonging to the 507th and 508th, beat down th[e]
Germans on either bank long enough to take the bridge — briefly. The Krau[ts]
soon gained the upper hand and retook it in see-saw fighting. They were n[ot]
permanently evicted until mid-day on the 9th, D + 3. The original battalio[n]
C.O., Maj. F.C. Kellam, and his successor, Maj. James McGinty, both pe[r]
ished in the D-Day battles.

Very tired 101 men and their adopted Sd. Kfz. 2 "Kettenkraftrad," a tracked motorcycle cargo carrier, in Isigny, 14 June 1944. The haggard dogface on the left
wears a gas-detector sleeve. (U.S. Army)

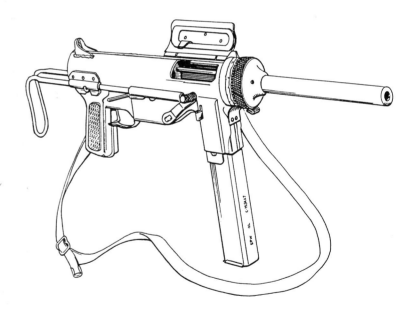

The M-3 submachine gun was inspired by the British STEN. Nicknamed th[e]
"Grease Gun," it was created by industrial engineers at the Inland Division [of]
General Motors, and made by the automaker's Guide Lamp Division. First issue[d]
overseas in late 1943 to units in England preparing for Normandy, problems wi[th]
case hardening, magazines and ejectors led to little use by the Airborne durin[g]
OVERLORD. Though very reliable (once fixed), its slow rate of fire and inacc[u]
racy foreclosed popularity with infantrymen, and Thompsons remained the pr[e]
ferred type.

The 2/505 did better in the drop, but its concentration and extraordinarily good communications ironically worked against it! Its commander, Lt. Col. Benjamin Vandervoort, was injured in the jump and had to lead his unit from a cart pulled by paratroopers. The unit's planned move from the DZ to the settlement of Neuville-au-Plain was delayed. There had been no word from the 3/505 as to the status of its higher-priority job of taking the town St. Mere-Eglise. Vandervoort received word (from Matt Ridgway himself, who had made the fifth parachute jump of his life with the 505th) to stand by for use there. But then it was put on the road to Neuville after all. Before getting there, the radios brought new word: turn around and head for St. Mere-Eglise! In one of the better decisions of a bad day, Vandervoort split off one rifle platoon (led by Lt. Turnbull) and sent it on into Neuville anyway. This small unit was fated to run into a much larger enemy force. In an epic stand, Turnbull's men held and squelched a Nazi flanking movement.

In town, Vandervoort found Lt. Col. Edward Krause and his incommunicado 3rd Battalion, alive and more or less well. Krause was delighted to see them, as he expected a serious battle to keep the place and soon. His own unit had nearly as good a drop as the 2/505 and had managed to infiltrate the crossroads municipality before dawn, then clear it from the inside out. The only artillery of the 82nd to parachute into Normandy — a two-gun section of the 456th PFAB — was attached to 3/505, but its fate is unrecorded.

The 507th PIR had drawn the job of blocking the westward approaches to the Merderet, on the far shore. But this regiment was damned to suffer the worst of any in the drop. Just two of its sticks landed on DZ "T" near Amfreville. Twelve others were strewn about within 20 miles. Most of the remaining 25 or so were dumped into the river or its bordering marshes. Not primed for water landings, many "Spidermen" tragically drowned, pushed to the bottom by the weight of their loads and hog-tied by the shroud lines of their parachutes. Commander Col. George Millett searched for his men for two days before being captured. While some of his far-flung sticks had the satisfaction of sowing terror in the enemy rear, only a few company-sized agglomerations of the 507th PIR functioned on D-Day. And these were mixed into "casual" groups dominated by men of other outfits.

In the 508th PIR's sector, bad drops tossed the plan right out the window. A grand total of seven sticks were on DZ "N," north of Picauville. Regimental commander Col. Roy Lindquist splashed down in the marshes to watch a flurry of equipment bundles settle into deeper water. The balance of his unit was plunked down everywhere but on the DZ. Many landed in the strongly defended areas south and east of Picauville, others east of the river. Perversely, the most concentrated drop deposited nine sticks atop one of the beach causeways, with a grandstand view of the amphibious landings. This was well within 101st territory and but a few short steps from a watery grave. Left to their own devilish devices, stray "Red Devils" raised hob. One typical episode was the impromptu ambush of the car carrying the boss of the Wehrmacht's 91st Infantry Division. In another free-for-all 2nd Battalion commander Lt. Col. John Shanley pulled together a hodgepodge of about 200 men and headed for the Pont L'Abbe bridge. Denied access by numerous Nazis, he set up on the handiest high ground. This modest hillock was Hill 30, from which repeated German attempts to punch a hole in the Airborne's thin perimeter were thwarted. The stand here proved essential in the survival of the western airhead.

In the see-saw hedgerow fighting of the post-assault Normandy campaign, the paratroopers came to admire the tenacity and hitting power of their Gliderman compatriots. Here an M1917A1 water-cooled machine gun of the 325th GIR (probably Company H of the 2nd Battalion) does its share in heavy fighting near Montebourg Station, 11 June 1944. (82nd Airborne Division Museum)

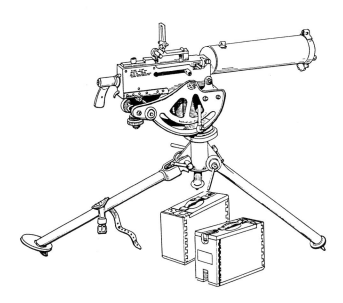

In the Airborne, the M1917A1 water-cooled .30 caliber machine gun was reserved for Gilder Infantry. By Normandy, the wooden ammo boxes had been supplanted by metal ones.

Screaming Eagles on the road to Carentan. Other than war souvenirs, these men haul an M-3A4 utility cart.

More warriors of the Eagle tribe on the warpath to Carentan. The truck seems populated by medics only, as no shoulder arms are to be seen. (U.S. Army)

Carentan, 14 June 1944. Three Screaming Eagles visit the landmark war memorial. Pvt. Charles Rinehart (left) drapes a Thompson mag bag across his belt while Sgt. James Long (center) seems to wear coveralls emblazoned with the 101st patch. A cleaning kit for machine guns hangs on his leg. Pvt. Charles We... has an extra pocket sewn to his sleeve and totes a machete.

On the glider side of D-Day operations, the 82nd was reinforced just prior to ~ybreak and twice again at dusk by missions routed from the east, over the ~aches and in plain view of aroused adversaries. In the predawn landings, ~ Waco CG-4A's (substituted for the heavier, faster-landing British Horsa ~en the mission was rescheduled into the hours of darkness) were to bring ~two batteries of the 80th AAA/AT Battalion plus some command and signal ~rsonnel — 220 troops and 16 AT guns, plus jeeps and cargo. A total of ~landed on or near LZ "W," centered on Les Forges, and a few more were ~se. In a helter-skelter cast-off, most glider pilots descended by the free-~le method, guiding on the landmark that was Ste. Mere-Eglise and playing ~keeps tag with the glowing arcs of enemy tracers. Crack-ups were the ~e. "Rommel asparagus" obstacles skewered some, one collided with a ~rd of cows. But only three troops died and half the guns and jeeps were ~erable. No matter where they came to earth, the guns were giddily received ~the paratroopers and fast put into vengeful action.

The evening glider mission involved 22 Wacos and 54 Horsas, flying in one ~, and a follow-up of 14 Wacos and 86 Horsas. In addition to another AT ~ttery, HQ, recdon, and support teams — 437 men, 64 jeeps, 13 guns, and ~ggage — were carried on the first. Accurate ground fire complicated this ~ylight lift. Ridgway had decided that LZ "W" was too hot and had moved ~ Pathfinders two miles to DZ "O." Alack, their signals were confused with

Carentan, 12 June 1944. Glidermen watch the passing parade: a jeep and gun of the 81st Airborne AAA Battalion. (U.S. Army)

T-5 James G. Pinelli and Lt. William I. Jones, Service Company, 501st PIR, stock up on souvenir German paratrooper helmets left behind by the 6th Fallschirmjager-Regiment, which had thrown itself against both the 82nd and 101st from Ste. Mere-Eglise to Carentan. (101st Airborne Division Association)

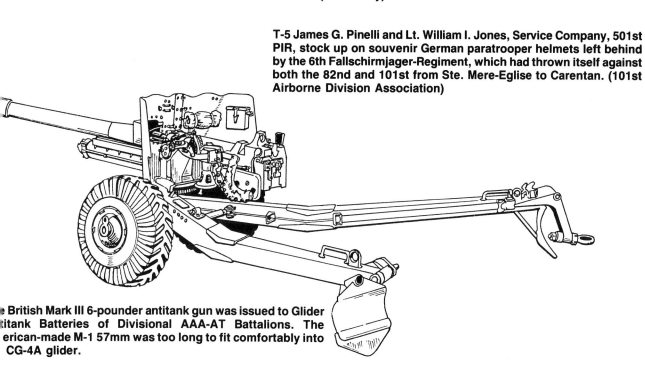

~e British Mark III 6-pounder antitank gun was issued to Glider ~titank Batteries of Divisional AAA-AT Battalions. The ~erican-made M-1 57mm was too long to fit comfortably into CG-4A glider.

Chaplain George "Chappie" Wood, who made four combat jumps, at Ste. Mere-Eglise.

This bunch (probably from the 101st) was captured near Orglandes (west of Ste. Mere-Eglise), but liberated soon after. Brandishing war souvenirs are Sgt. Robert B. Utley, Cpl. Frank Kwasnik, Pvt. Frank Rupper, Sgt. Orlando Peters, Lt. Briand M. Beaudin, and Lt. Paul E. Lehman. (Dick Reardon)

others set out for unrelated missions, and with those set out by personnel on LZ "W." The latter included a seaborne detachment of the 82nd, under Col. Edson Raff, consisting of a company of the 325th Glider Infantry and attachments. They thought the area too warm and tried to warn off the incoming bunch. Under trying circumstances, 25 gliders realized on LZ "W" didn't seem too bad. Another 18 crunched in close by, and a dozen Horsas chose the nearby LZ "E" of the 101st. The next lift delivered the 319th and 320th Glider Field Artillery Battalions and support personnel at nightfall.

Like the preceding wave, this one was unaware of Ridgway's changes — it approached LZ "W" in good order at 2255 hours. German fire was heavy enough to cause early releases, putting most of the 319th GFAB two miles out of the LZ. Eleven went astray and five settled on the LZ. Due to holed and wrecked equipment, neither Redleg unit was able to use its howitzers soon. The 319th eventually got six of its 75mm howitzers on the job, and the 320th eight of its 105mm's, but only by late on D + 2.

On the morrow of D + 1, the All-American received more gliderborne reinforcements. The 1st Battalion and HQ of the 325th GIR and miscellaneous elements came in on zones "E" and "W" via 82 Wacos and 18 Horsas. Only a too-low and too-soon release (of gliders loaded in excess of usual norms) causing an on-zone demolition derby at "E" disturbed at textbook-perfect operation. The 2/325 and 2/401 (alias 3/325) skidded in two hours later in much the same fashion, save a few that landed amidst Wehrmacht soreheads and drew some wrath. A comparatively huge fighting force, the 325th GIR was quickly sent on to chase Germans impeding the 4th Infantry Division and thence to divisional reserve.

Like the 82nd, Maj. Gen. Maxwell Taylor's 101st Airborne Division h been rearranged for Normandy. In addition to its original 502nd PIR, and 506th PIR it had taken along overseas for reinforcement, it had acquired other one-time subordinate of the 2nd Airborne Brigade, the 501st PIR. round out the ensemble, the Screaming Eagles also included the 327th Gli Infantry. Even though the 82nd had divorced itself from its second glider re ment — the 320th — when it was about to deploy from the States, the 10 had brought its other GIR along. The 401st GIR, however, was chopped in for OVERLORD. Its 1st Battalion (GIR's had only two by the definition then c rent) stayed more or less put, but was appended to the 327th as the so-ca "3rd Battalion, 327th GIR." In like fashion, the 2/401 was sent packing to 82nd to assume the identity "3/325th." Troops became so used to these sanctioned redesignations in ensuing months, it was not until 6 April 1945, t paperwork made these marriages permanent and official. As the staff of out-of-a-job 2nd Airborne Brigade had melted into the HQ of the 82nd, the he quarters people of the 401st augmented the 101st overhead.

Where the mission of the 82nd was to get across the bridges and h the line on the north and west, the 101st was charged with securing the rou of egress from UTAH beach and the southeast edge of the lodgement, cluding grabbing at least one end of the spans over the Douve. The "Ger imo" 501st (the eldest Parachute Infantry unit of all) was to take the r locks and deny bridges to the enemy. Its drop was scattered, but few co plained once they comprehended the projected DZ "D" was so obvious the Germans that they had set it up as a killing-ground trap. Regimental cc mander Howard "Jumpy" Johnson took charge of 1st Battalion eleme

When the battle for the hedgerows ebbed, Omar Bradley visited the 82nd to present medals. Lt. Col. Benjamin Vandervoort (with cane) had commanded the 2d Battalion of the 505th PIR at Ste. Mere-Eglise. (Dick Reardon)

By the helmet marks, these are 3/502nd PIR men, hence paratroopers — yet they carry non-folding carbines and wear "leg" clothing. Dating the picture is made difficult by the buckled combat boots, which were first issued in quantity in August 1944 — the same time the M1941 ensemble was being withdrawn. (101st Airborne Division Association)

leaderless after the death of Lt. Col. Robert Carroll, the capture of his XO, and the disappearance of four company commanders — in the neighborhood of the DZ. He forthwith superintended the seizure of the locks at La Barquette and got a paradropped naval gunfire officer busy, ringing up the cruiser USS QUINCY for some salvos. This heartening firepower was turned against sources of enemy fire and the Carentan bridges, but the latter could not be knocked out so simply.

The 2nd Battalion descended in clusters around the DZ, well away from its objective, the Carentan bridges. Lt. Col. Robert Ballard managed to round up a fair number of his men — many soaked and minus gear from water landings — but could not break contact near the Les Droueries farmstead to move to the bridges. The Germans kept them until 10 June.

The 3/501st led by Lt. Col. Julian Ewell had jumped with the majority of the 506th on DZ "C." It had been tasked as the Division reserve and was to prepare the overlapping LZ "E" for the later glider landings. Despite losses to flak, most of the battalion was able to concentrate on the LZ. But General Taylor feared the 506th would be unable to fulfill its obligations at the beach exit at Pouppeville, and bid Ewell to head there.

Due to a broken leg, Col. George Moseley turned his 502nd PIR over to his exec, Lt. Col. "Mike" Michaelis. Widely spread out and intermixed with other units in the drop, the plan for the regiment was to neutralize a battery of Russian-made cannon ranged in on the beaches and tie down the north flank.

Lt. Col. Pat Cassidy's 1st Battalion fared relatively well in the jump — though one planeload had landed in the Channel and drowned to a man. Once it was clear that Germans were not contesting the beach exits that were his first order of business, Cassidy cast about for other jobs for his troops. In one episode, SSgt. Harrison Summers of Company B, sporadically helped by a mixed bag of paratroopers from other units who happened to pass by, killed or capatured 150 Wehrmacht artillerymen in a barracks complex at Mesieres. At Foucarville and Haut Fornel, Cassidy's marauders had a field day; their efforts on the flank of the beachhead were later assessed as the most important tactical accomplishment of the 101st on D-Day. In a typical event, German convoy hellbent to join the fight at the shore blundered into a roadblock and was wiped out. Other troopers, with Cassidy, hied themselves to the Varreville battery, only to find a contingent of the 2nd Battalion already there — and no artillery pieces. These things accomplished, the 1/502 dug in to await developments.

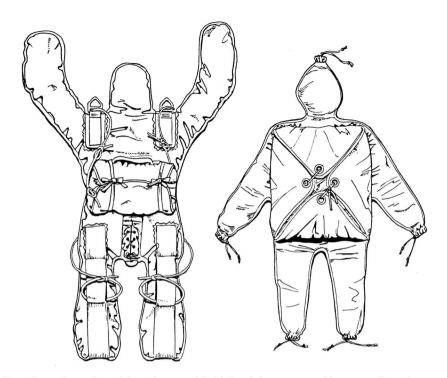

Parachute dummies of American and British origin were used in many diversionary airdrops. The former were assembled by the Switlik Parachute Company under Navy contract. Their "PD (parachute dummy) Pack" had a four-foot rubber inflatable with Mark 112 Demolition Outfit on its chest, folded up inside a small parachute pack. A static-line deployed the canopy, opened a carbon dioxide bottle, and actuated a three-minute delay fuse. TNT blocks, primacord loops, and a multiple-charge train to simulate gunfire combined to stir up defenders and destroy the evidence of a ruse. The simpler British "TITANIC" was made of burlap or canvas, filled with straw or excelsior, folded and tied in a bundle that opened when strings were snapped by the rip cord. A 20-minute-maximum adjustable delay simulator — a separate piece — was pitched out the door with each "stick." Either type could be dressed in cast-off uniforms for enhanced realism. Only the British model was used in Normandy and Holland, while the American style is known to have been used in Southern France and the Philippines. (Courtesy R.W. Koch)

Lt. Col. Steve Chappuis' 2/502 had an enjoyable, compact drop. The problem was that they wound up on the wrong DZ! Instead of DZ "A," they were more than three miles removed, on "C." Starting with just a dozen prodigals, Chappuis struck off in the direction of his objective: the guns at Varreville. But the position had been vacated days before, then clobbered from the air. As more battalion men drifted in, they dug into the still-smoking soil.

The 3/502 suffered a very poor drop, with Lt. Col. Robert Cole landing among 82nd people near Ste. Mere-Eglise. Cole gathered in whatever paratroopers he encountered on his hike toward Varreville — and tore up a German column en route. Upon seeing the defanged battery, he split up his

variegated force to cover Exits 3 and 4 from the beach, suspecting that t[h]e Boche from forward positions would soon decide to call it quits and com[e] his way. The results were 75 dead Krauts in the first exchange of fire. Col[e]['s] saga was remarkable in that his enthusiastic and efficient force had few me[n] from his own regiment, let alone his own battalion. Perhaps half were 82n[d] members.

The 377th Parachute Field Artillery Battalion that normally supported t[he] 502nd PIR was at this time the sole Parachute cannoneer unit in the 101s[t]. It was largely frustrated in its intentions on D-Day. In the early stages, ju[st] one of its pack 75's could be put into action. Though a total of six (and [a] captured German 105) were operating late in the day, by then the bigge[st] cluster of its personnel were fighting as riflemen — or rather as tommygu[n]ners and carabiniers, as they were not armed with rifles.

The 506th PIR (nicknamed the "Five-O-Sink" in honor of its command[er], Col. Robert Sink) was another one widely dispersed. Only ten sticks we[re] on DZ "C," between Hiesville and Exit 1. Unable to attack the planned o[b]jectives of Exits 1 and 2 and the Douve bridges near Le Port, Sink impr[o]vised. He sent his 1st Battalion commander, Lt. Col. William Turner, and [?] soldiers to Exit 1 (where they found the 3/501 had the situation well in han[d]). Gen. Taylor travelled with the 506th, becoming — by moments — the fir[st] general officer to make a combat jump (his second jump ever).

Intended for that Exit, the 2nd Battalion of Lt. Col. Robert Strayer wa[s] subjected to a strung-out jump that put most of its fighters far to the nor[th] near Foucarville. This group of 200-plus headed south. At Exit 4, it overcan[e] a Nazi strongpoint, but then ran up against another at Exit 3. To reduce th[at] one, Capt. Winters of Company E rustled up a few friendly tanks from UTA[H] beach. By afternoon, the 2/506 moved further on to occupy Exit 2 and li[ned] up with 3/501 at Exit 1.

The hardest luck in the 101st befell the 3/506 under Lt. Col. Robert Wol[v]erton. Split from its parent unit and cross-attached to the 501st to grab t[he] Le Port bridges, it also landed in the middle of the German trap at DZ "D[."] Among those cut down in moments by the crossfire were Wolverton and h[is] deputy. It fell to the unit's operations officer, Capt. Charles Shettle, to car[ry] on. From those who survived and others found lurking on the edges, he pull[ed] together 54 troopers. Against opposition, they forced one of the bridges a[nd] got a party to the far shore, but lack of communications and ammo thwart[ed] exploitation.

Glider elements of the 101st played only minor roles on D-Day. Befo[re] dawn, two batteries of the 81st Airborne AAA/AT Battalion plus staff, engine[er,] signal and medical elements — amounting to 155 personnel, 25 jeeps, o[ne] midget bulldozer, and 16 6-pounder guns — took off in 52 Wacos. One, carryi[ng] the Division headquarters' radio set, parted tow near the departure field; t[he] signalmen hurriedly headed back to the airfield, hired another aircraft, a[nd] joined a later airlift. Despite an orderly Pathfinder reception, mishaps c[ut] arrivals on or near LZ "E" to just 21 gliders, shortly after 0400 hours. T[wo] more alit nearly two miles away at Les Forges and the remaining 18 we[re] everywhere and nowhere. Due to the dark, crisscross hedgerows, tall tre[es] and uneven ground, most gliders were rendered hors d'combat on landi[ng.] Death claimed Assistant Division Commander Brig. Gen. Don Pratt, the fir[st]

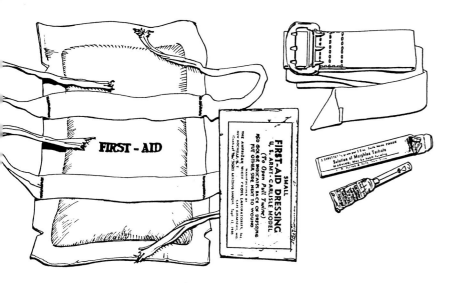

e Kit, First Aid, Parachute was issued with parachutes, firstly to USAAF air-w personnel, secondarily to paratroops. Its tie-tapes facilitated attachment parachute harnesses, but Airborne soldiers — wanting to keep it with them er parting company with their chutes — affixed it anywhere they could. The berized cloth packet contained a "Carlisle" or "shell" dressing, a web torni-et and a styrette of morphine.

heral to make a combat glider landing. In a typical crack-up — unable to ke on a field of soggy grass and mud — his Waco had plowed into the cage at 50 mph, crushing him between a jeep and cargo that broke loose.

In the summer twilight, a later glider mission using 32 Horsas brought 150-plus troops, vehicles, cargo, and more AT guns. Glider pilots of the lier lift and Pathfinders had improved the LZ a bit and everything went e — until the cast-off at 2053 hours. Germans who had held their fire then ened up, killing 14 Yanks, wounding or injuring 30 more, and sieving many lers.

But the 101st's glider missions included no combat troops. The 327th GIR ived by boat. The 1/401 sloshed across the beaches on D-Day, but enemy istance stymied its planned link-up with the 506th until midnight of D + 1. e division's 321st and 907th GFAB's were delayed by the sinking of a troop nsport and resulting problems of reuniting rescued personnel, cadres, and uipment. Until these outfits (and a 377th PFAB given replacement guns those lost in the drop) entered the fray on D + 4, the 101st was supported borrowed self-propelled 105's. Two .50 caliber AAMG batteries of the 81st A/AT hit the beach late on D-Day and scored against two Luftwaffe planes. AT battery accompanied the 327th ashore, and Division rear echelon as-s debarked on D + 3.

For all its shortcomings, post mortems of the OVERLORD Airborne ssion showed that the Airborne was suitable for division-sized commit-ints, providing it was massed on critical terrain and within link-up

distance of heavier forces. After-action reports also underlined the criticality of careful preparations and comprehensive planning, especially for airlift and Pathfinders — on the Murphy's Law model! Past mistakes had been avoided, and losses were much less than foretold by some doomsayers. Placed where heavy German resistance was anticipated, the Airborne was successful in protecting the 4th Infantry Division as it landed on UTAH beach. At OMAHA beach, where no sky soldiers ran interference, the invaders fought desper-ately for every inch of sand, with high losses and no artillery or heavy gear put ashore. While not a cure-all, large Airborne operations were thereafter seen as a vital part of major assaults.

In the weeks following the landings, the Airborne fought on through the Norman countryside. On D + 1 at La Fiere, a piece of the 505th parried a Ger-man thrust led by two 1940 vintage Renault tanks. At an interval of less than 50 yards, a ferocious firefight broke out. The senior officer present, Lt. Dolan, met talk of withdrawal with a stoic, "I don't know a better spot to die." After a truce to tend to dead and wounded on both sides, these "Panthers" were relieved by a force of regrouped 507th "Spiders." A provisional battalion of the 507th was also added to the force holding Ste. Mere-Eglise against con-tinued Nazi attentions, and a third bunch isolated west of the Merderet be-tween Amfreville and Le Motey (under 2/507 commander Lt. Col. Charles Timmes) was joined by the 1/325th GIR under Maj. Teddy Sanford.

Efforts to force a crossing at La Fiere were resumed on D + 2 by the 507th group, 2/401, Sherman tanks and artillery support from the 90th Infantry Di-vision. Two companies of glidermen dashed onto the narrow causeway and took heavy losses in a bloody baptism of fire. Its third company and A/507 pushed through the melee, set up positions on the far side, and gradually rooted out the Huns.

Back at Ste. Mere-Eglise, repeated attacks were beaten off, but the issue remained in doubt until Col. Raff's group, the 8th Infantry Regiment of the 4th Infantry Division, and tanks dissuaded the besiegers. On D + 3 the Ameri-cans pushed north to Monteville, Le Ham, and Mountebourg. The 508th crossed the Douve ten days later to link up with the 101st. The rest of the All-Americans moved west to cut off the Contentin peninsula. After battles at St. Sauveur-le-Vicomte and Le Haye de Puits, 33 days in the line, and more than half its infantrymen casualties, the 82nd was relieved.

After cleaning out St. Come-du-Mont and sorting out its order of battle, the 101st pushed into Carentan to meet the OMAHA beach units. One high-light of this phase was the 3/502 fight at Bridge 4. Commander Lt. Col. Cole faced a storm of fire from a farmhouse and called for an all-out charge to overwhelm the defenders. At his signal, Cole charged. But the din of battle had prevented the passing of the word — he and a few other lonely chargers were out in the storm by themselves. But all was not lost — the rest soon got the idea and the Krauts were overrun. Cole's action earned the Medal of Honor, but he never got to wear it; a sniper killed him in Holland.

Carentan fell on D + 6, but the Screaming Eagles got no respite. German counterattacks were met in toe-to-toe violence and the town stayed in Allied hands. After mopping up, the 101st moved west to back up units pounding Cherbourg on 27 June. When it redeployed to England beginning on 10 July, it had suffered 4,670 casualties, compared to 5,245 in the 82nd.

OSS: OUTRAGEOUS SECRET SOLDIERS

The Office of Strategic Services, the first national-level intelligence agency in the US, was the brainchild of William J. Donovan, a lawyer and colonel in the National Guard who had received the Congressional Medal of Honor in World War I. To detractors, it was "a fly-by-night civilian outfit headed by a wild man trying to horn in on the war."

The OSS was therefore less and more than a military organization. Its basic purpose was to consolidate intelligence, transcending both the War and Navy Departments. By charter, it was temporary — an adjunct of the Executive Office of the President, created to supplement the usual Cabinet Departments for the duration of the war.

Established 13 June 1942, it supplanted the civil Office of the Coordinator of Information Donovan had headed since 11 July 1941. It was thereafter a "supplemental activity" of the Joint Chiefs of Staff, and began looking like a military organization. Eventually about 9,000 of the 13,000 OSS personnel were military — some of them "civilians in disguise," some soldiers for the duration, but very few of them professional military men.

By the time of the North African campaign, OSS was reaching into the realm of combat. Its main operational arms were the Secret Intelligence and Special Operations Branches. SI, most active prior to invasion, collected intelligence covertly. Its agents were spies, in civilian clothes and carrying bogus identities, liable to execution when caught. The operatives of SO were saboteurs, out to destroy military or economic targets; even when uniformed, the enemy seldom deemed them legitimate combatants.

Through 1943, OSS built strength. Contacts with the undergrounds on the Continent encouraged planners to take Churchill's plea to "set Europe ablaze" to heart. Yet the task of guerrilla warfare needed more soldierly skills — and many more skilled soldiers — than SI and SO had. "Fomentors and nuclei of guerrilla units" or "Raiders" had long been Donovan's dream, and had been authorized by the JCS on 23 December 1942. Yet the Operational Groups Branch was not embodied until 4 May 1943.

The OG's, the most military elements of OSS, were by function the ancestors of Army Special Forces: volunteers, fluent in foreign languages, skilled in weapons, demolition, scouting and survival. Usually, but not always, they were parachute-qualified, with many recruited from Airborne units. On paper, the OG Branch was separate and distinct from the spies and saboteurs, to sustain claims that its troops were entitled to Geneva Convention status if captured. An OG had a theoretical strength of 34 men, subdivided into two Sections, each about 15 strong. In practice (and varying with timeframe and theater), individuals moved easily between SO and OG teams, and forces of more than 100 OG men — augmented with SI/SO specialists and Allies — were assembled for some missions.

The combat debut of the OG's came with the capitulation of Italy in September 1943. Prior to then, resistance to the Fascist regime was small, but the turnabout and German reprisals changed all. The first OG section parachuted into Sardinia on the 12th, accompanying an SO team. Five days later, an entire OG, with SI attachments and Free French troops, went ashore to liberate Corsica.

Venafro, spring 1944: Lt. DeSalvo, Tech. Sgts. Ets Galassi and Stelvio Silva of Company D, 2677th OSS Regiment. Note the modified British battledress (with snaps replacing buttons), "pink" officers' overseas cap, jump wings worn o the pocket, and jump trousers. (Ets Galassi)

The well-dressed OSS man in Italy: In February 1945, Capt. Bill DeSalvo spor a custom-tailored "PARACHUTE" tab above the Fifth Army patch. The numbe "313" above his crossed rifles are not a disinformation ploy — they are leftove from his days as a "shavetail" Lieutenant in the 79th Infantry Division. (Willia J. DeSalvo, Jr.)

In Europe, the Year of the OG's was 1944. The *Maquis* had an essenti role in the invasions of Normandy and southern France. Command and co trol of OG's (as well as SO and the British SOE) was vested in two inter-Allie centers formed on 1 May: for the north, Special Forces Headquarters (SFH(in England, for the south of France the Special Projects Operational Cent (SPOC) in Algiers. SO/SOE dominated ops in the north, with just seven OG inserted by SFHQ. SPOC committed 14 OG Sections (182 US troops).

In the Mediterranean Theater of Operations, OSS was large enough organize on military lines. The overall OSS command for the MTO, the 2677 Headquarters Company (Provisional), was formed at Algiers on 1 April 194 (a month before OG Branch back in Washington). Collocated with it we.

mpanies A, B, and C. These were responsible for dispatching and supporting SI, SO and OG teams, plus supplying the materiel for their local associates, in southern France, Italy, and Yugoslavia, respectively.

This lineup sufficed until 11 May 1944. For expanded operations, the 2677th came an OSS Regiment, commanded by the senior OSS man in MTO HQ. ce moved closer to the action, at Caserta, Italy, it was subordinated to 15th Army Group and reorganized. Its HQ and HQ Company paired the ual service elements with OSS specific Morale Operations, Research and alysis, Counter-intelligence (X-2), and Co-Belligerent Italian staffs. Added the older organic units, Company D was tasked with forward support of US Fifth and British Eighth Armies. From the friendly side of the battles, it coordinated partisans and spies.

On 4 May 1943, "Operational Group, Fifth Army" had been split from 677. On 1 August 1944, it and the OG's of all the old companies became anic to the new 2671st Special Reconnaissance Battalion (Provisional). vas comprised of Company A for Italy, Company B for southern France, d Company C for Yugoslavia. The 2671st was attached to the 2677th. aller units under the 2677th included the Maritime Unit (later a Detachnt with Company D) and the Independent American Military Mission to Tito.

The war in Yugoslavia was an especially complicated affair. The British ght US involvement there and insisted all support be thrown to the Comnist partisans and none to the Chetniks. A cooperative, combined HQ was viable. Yet the biggest OG units fought there, in pitched battles. By Sepber 1944, 15 OG teams had been inserted. In December, German attacks the major support base on the liberated island of Vis were beaten off by, r alia, 211 OG soldiers. With British Commandos, 150 OG's and 450 parns assailed Solta, Brac and other isles in Dalmatia.

The OSS base in Egypt, the 2791st Operations and Training Unit (Proonal), was within the MTO and also reported to the 2677th. For OG work Greece, it controlled the 122nd Infantry Battalion, which was commonly wn by its cover name: "3rd Contingent, Unit B." This was an ethnic unit nposed of US citizens and aliens who spoke Greek. When OSS had visthe unit at Camp Carson, Colorado, looking for volunteers for dangerous sions behind enemy lines, the whole unit stepped forward! Eventually, 222

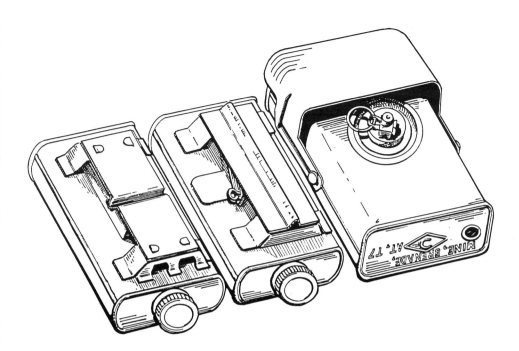

The British Hawkins Mine (Grenade Number 76) often employed by parachute troops was set off by a crush fuze. Early on it was deemed adequate to blow treads off tanks, but by 1944 it was not enough and it found application as an anti-truck mine and railroad track demolition. The Mark II (left) was followed by the Improved Mark III. The US developed the bigger T-7, packed with Composition C, but even it was not often successful against tanks. It could fit in the leg pocket on a jump suit, and was a favorite of OSS men.

most common suppressed pistol used by the OSS was the Hi-Standard H-D 22 Long Rifle caliber. The High Standard firm's main business was machine ls, but in 1932 it inherited the "Model A" pistol design when its client, the tford Arms and Equipment Company, went bankrupt. The later Model B was dified with an exposed hammer and safety switch to become the H-B. After ring some of these types off-the-shelf, the Military took the lion's share of duction between March 1942 and May 1945. Among the 40,000 military Hindards were about 2,500 with suppressors for the OSS. Beginning in April 3, Bell Laboratories modified over 100 civilian-type Hi-Standards and Colts silencers. These prototypes were followed by two lots from the High Standfactory. Between January and March 1944, 1,500 were delivered, and 1,000 he September-December period. Most if not all were the Model H-D, by then latest version, with heavy barrel and horizontal butt. In late 1944, the OSS ed for a variant in .380 ACP caliber, but only one prototype was delivered ore cancellation of the contract; in the post-war era it appeared as a civilian del. (Information courtesy Dr. John Brunner)

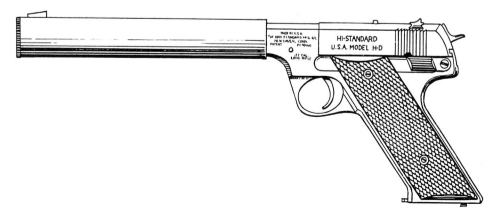

These rare (and unidentified) photos from the papers of an American pilot who flew "CARPETBAGGER" sorties show groups of "Joes" embarking for insertion in occupied France in mid-1944. British-kitted French SAS men with American carbines and a Thompson in a C-47 (note the stretchers for medical evacuation missions) on an air-landing trip. A bon voyage, apparently the same mission. A team of Yanks — possibly OG's — wearing brand-new M1943 field jackets and the odd combination of British Type X main chutes with added-on reserves.

As a covert entity, the Office of Strategic Services had no reason to adopt organizational insignia for the uniforms of its military personnel. However, as the war wore on, the OSS became more overt, and a change of heart inspired the black and gold emblems. Not officially authorized by the War Department, fewer than 200 shoulder sleeve insignia were made under contract in the U.S. during the war. The enamelled metal badge was worn at least on shirt collars — in the fashion of officers' "U.S." brass displayed by Counter-Intelligence Corps agents — to conceal actual rank and confer quasi-officer status.

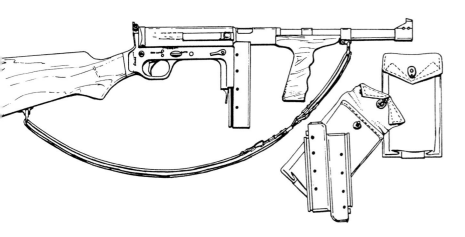

The United Defense M42 submachine gun was a 9mm weapon, designed by High Standard but manufactured by Marlin. Aimed at foreign sales, a few hundred were delivered to the Dutch West Indies, but most of the 15,000 made passed into the hands of OSS and thence to guerrillas in Greece, Yugoslavia, China, Thailand and possibly other areas. Its 20-round magazines were similar to the Thompson's, but not interchangeable. Pairs soldered together could be carried in the unmarked commercial-style pouch shown.

were selected for OSS, of which 180 deployed as a unit to Egypt. Infiltration of Greece started on 23 April 1944. Few of the over 200 OG troops inserted by the 2791st were paradropped; the normal mode of travel was sailboats on a circuitous route via Alexandria, Cyprus and Turkey. Their greatest achievements came in a bitter campaign against lines of communications when the Germans were trying to evacuate — Operation SMASHEM, begun on 8 September.

The most ambitious OSS-sponsored guerrilla war in Europe was in the highland areas of southeastern France. From the time the Germans swallowed Vichy, maquisards thirsting for revenge gathered there in mountain bastions. On 6 January, an SFHQ SO/SOE "Jedburgh" team dubbed UNION jumped into one of these areas, the Haute-Savoie department bordering Switzerland and Italy. London did not then realize the size of the "Secret Army." The UNION men meant only to assess but it proved too late in the deadly game to get in and out without fighting, and clashes with the occupiers ensued. Unfortunately, UNION was not positioned to help when hundreds of *Maquis* on the Glieres plateau were encircled and crushed in March. In May, as the blood of martyrs and anticipation of invasion brought forth thousands of new volunteers, UNION was withdrawn by night-landing Lysanders.

UNION's American was Marine Captain Peter Ortiz, fated to be a legend. He had been in the Foreign Legion and was severely wounded and captured in 1940. He escaped in Austria, made his way to Paris and Portugal, and was bound for home when he heard of Pearl Harbor. He tried to enlist in the USMC, but had to wait until he healed. In boot camp as a private, he was marked for parachute duty and a commission; then Naval Intelligence claimed him.

Maj. J.W. Summer of the OSS — probably a Jedburgh team member — wears the special Force wings in the field, somewhere near Brest, September 1944.

In January 1943, he was a naval attache to London — only to wend his way to the front of Algeria and combat with SOE. Wounded, decorated, and promoted, he then settled in with OSS.

During UNION, he had found himself drinking with a group of Gestapo and French collaborators one evening. His perfect French and fair German saved him and he tarried to pick up information. Alas, his companions began berating the United States and President Roosevelt. When they insulted the Marine Corps, Ortiz excused himself. He returned to his safehouse, changed into his service greens, donned a raincoat and returned to the bistro. There, he removed his coat to

Americans and Norwegians of OSS Operational Group NORSO pose in Oslo, May 1945. In the months before V-E Day, Operation RYPE (named for an indigenous snow grouse) was to interdict the railway that sped Wehrmacht assets from the battlefront in Finnmark to the Oslo area, where ferries took them to ports in Germany for use in the climactic fight for the Reich. It had only "mixed success," the good parts springing from the dedication and initiative of the operatives led by Maj. William Colby (later the director of the CIA). Several wear SF wings; one Norwegian wears the GQ para wing. (William C. Colby)

The first parachutist brevet worn by British paras was this lapel pin given [by] the GQ parachute company. Once the official qualification wing was appro[ved] (about December 1940), the GQ wing was rarely seen.

reveal his true identity. With a .45 in each hand, he then demanded the enemy to toast America, Roosevelt, and the Corps. Getting compliance, he exited, guns blazing, and escaped into the night.

The Germans had not heard the last of the *Maquis* in southern France. Their problem only grew. In early June, the FFI wreaked serious damage and delay on the 2nd SS Panzer Division "Das Reich" as it tried to reach Normandy. In retribution, the SS committed atrocities, among them the obliteration of the innocent town of Ouradour-sur-Glane.

Late in the month, SPOC sent new teams, JUSTINE (OG), EUCALYPTUS (SOE), and PAQUEBOT (French) to continue supplying and training the growing army of insurrectionists. At the Vercors plateau town of Vassieux, an airstrip was readied to receive C-47's. This was the DZ for the first daylight aerial resupply mission on 25 June. Operation CADILLAC, a larger drop on Bastille Day, 14 July, like the Glieres episode, drew the wrath of the Nazis to the zealous, imprudent *maquisards.* This counterstroke was bigger and bolder than before — the "Das Reich" debacle had brought higher priorities for counter-guerrilla ops. German planes strafed and bombed, the colored cargo chutes their reference points. Two divisions — 20,000 troops including 20 gliders full of SS men making the airstrip their LZ — gained the upper hand and gave no quarter. With heavy losses, they managed to scatter the FFI main force. The mop-up saw massacres of prisoners and civilians. The Nazis proclaimed the Haute-Savoie Resistance dead.

Then Peter Ortiz returned, with a few friends. On 1 August came *le Gra[nd] Parachutage,* the largest air resupply to the FFI. Jumping singly from am[ong] the 78 B-17's that disgorged over 800 containers of arms and gear for a fo[rce] of 3,000 were the seven members of UNION II. Six were Marines, one Arm[y] Sergeant Charles Perry, USMC, died when his static line cable kinked; [his] British chute failed and he had no reserve.

This time the *Maquis* did well. In Haute-Savoie and other areas, ene[my] columns racing to the DZ's were ambushed. The abundant supplies w[ere] expeditiously picked up and sent on to waiting customers. The FFI had fin[ally] learned; rather than hold ground, they hit hard and melted away. So stro[ng] had they become in mere months, they materially assisted the advance [of] the Allies from the Riviera. The DRAGOON plans had envisioned taking th[ree] months to advance as far as Grenoble; with the FFI's help, it took one we[ek.] Seemingly everywhere, the *Maquis* eventually cut off nearly 100,000 N[azi] troops near Limoges; there were too many of them for the Frenchmen to e[xe]cute in retribution, and their OSS/SOE associates pressed to keep them a[live] as POW's.

With the Germans stirred up, the UNION II OG's fared less well. Try[ing] to evade the hot DZ area and reach outlying FFI units, they were spot[ted] by the Wehrmacht. The fox-and-hounds chase that followed ended 10 da[ys] later. Cornered in a town, Ortiz and two other Marines fought ferociou[sly] but they could not hope to escape or win. Mindful of the foe's habit of wip[ing] out villages, Ortiz suggested they forego a fight to the death (theirs) in ret[urn] for leaving the place in peace. The German commander accepted — his loss[es] convinced him these *amis* amounted to a full company of paras. In their c[on]fusion, the captors treated the trio as true POW's, presuming them to be w[ay]ward invaders from the DRAGOON landings then taking place.

OG's as such had begun arriving in China the month before and were charged with training and advising a force of over 1,000 airborne-qualified Chinese Commandos. The pre-existing Nationalist 1st Parachute Regiment proved to need wholesale remedial attention. After three months of effort, the 1st-4th and 8th-10th Commandos — each numbering about 200 men and led by a 19-man OG — were ready for combat. After the 1st and 8th-10th had infiltrated the Kaiping and Liuchow areas, the 2nd made a parachute assault (Operation BLUEBERRY) at Chaking on 27 July. The 3rd (CHERRY) and 4th (CRABAPPLE) followed suit at Nanking airfield on 27 August.

OG personnel in China combat also included 13 teams inserted with guerrillas well behind Japanese lines and several MERCY teams that in August and September jumped into internment camps in Manchuria, Korea, and Shanghai to free prisoners and forestall Japanese atrocities. OG teams of all types operated under three area Field Commands (north of the Yangtze, south of it, and for Yunnan/Indo-China). Guerrilla teams usually had four Americans and a variable number of OSS-trained Chinese Commandos.

Members of OSS Team Union at Les Saisies, France, drop zone, August 2, 1944. Left to right: J.P. Bodnar; Major Peter Ortiz, USMC; Sgt. Bob LaSalle; Fritz Brunner, Capt. F. Collige; Sgt. Jack Risler, USMC. (Risler)

e baseball-like T-12 "Beano" grenade filled with Composition C was intended improve on the safety of the Gammon and capitalize on Americans' throwing lities. It was developed by the Eastman Kodak Corporation and first fielded h Airborne units in the ETO in late 1944. The improved T-13 was slightly larger d safer.

By early 1945 there was little for OG's to do in the ETO and MTO, and S began shifting resources to China, Burma, and Southeast Asia.

The OSS career in that region had begun in September 1942, when De- hment 101 (a randomly picked designation) was formed in Assam. Wash- ton OSS had sent it to work in China, but Lt. Gen. Stilwell did not want people sucked into the quagmire of intrigue that was Chinese intelligence. tead, "Vinegar Joe" asked 101 to build up a network for, firstly, intelli- nce collection and the exfiltration of downed aviators, and, secondarily, otage and guerrilla warfare inside Burma.

The Detachment was so successful that by December 1943 it had two anced bases operating inside Burma, and by the following spring, it had ruited an irregular army of perhaps 6,000 tribesmen. These were the "Ka- n Rangers" — renamed "Jingpaw Rangers" when it was determined that achin" was a deprecatory name used by other tribes for the warriors who led themselves "Jingpaw."

Formed as main-force Battalions and scout sections attached directly to rrill's Marauders, they facilitated the February-August 1944 offensive that minated in the conquest of Myitkyina. Thereafter, they were expanded ther for operations in northernmost Burma and the Shan States, reaching eak strength of 9,200 Jingpaws under arms and nearly 300 American cadre- n.

S.A.A.R.F.

Right to left: Polish, American, French and Dutch men of the Special Allied Airborne Rescue Force, at a disbandment party, 10 June 1945.

The SF wing began with the Inter-Allied Special Forces HQ set up in the United Kingdom in early 1944. M[...] a souvenir than a qualification badge or organizational emblem, it was variously purchased and worn at i[...] vidual option by ''Jedburghs'' of several nationalities, American OSS SO and OG personnel, and even aircre[...] who supported covert missions. The SAARF cuff badge was, like the SF wing, an anomalous ''souvenir'' w[...] by troops of several nations. The usage of the S.A.A.R.F. title is unknown.

Detachment 101 had no patience with the nuances of military organization and made no distinctions of SO, SI or OG. It grew from less than fifty Americans commanded by a Major into a multinational command of Division-size headed by a Colonel that was emulated by the organization of the Special Forces Groups of the 1950's. Under its control were little-known spin-off units: battalion-size Detachment 202 (with organic Dets 203-206), for ops inside China from early 1945; Det 303, a service unit in New Delhi; 404, another ''battalion,'' formed in June 1944 and credited with five assault landings in support of Commonwealth advances in Burma, Malaya and Thailand; and Det 505, the Calcutta base.

Before the advent of Det 202 and ''OSS China Combat Command,'' a precursor, the 5329th Provisional Unit (Air-Ground Forces Resources and Technical Staff), had been formed at 14th Air Force HQ in Kunming on 26 April 1944. Its peculiar name was a cover, but aimed at confusing the nefarious Chinese intelligence service, not the Japanese!

The sterling silver ''OSS Burma Bar'' was awarded to veterans of Detachme[...] 101 as an unofficial keepsake, but many proudly wore it on their uniforms. T[...] Chinese parachute wings in brass were allegedly designed by OSS OG advis[...] and more commonly worn by Americans than Chinese troops.

CHAMPAGNE AND TEARS: THE FORCE'S FINALE

The 1st Special Service Force and pieces of the 1st Armored Division led
[t]he mad dash to liberate Rome. In typical fashion, its commander evaded
[cr]owds of jubilant citizens in a borrowed halftrack to lead his "Black Devils"
[in] a run for the bridges that were their objective, getting his seventh and eighth
[wo]unds in a skirmish once there.

After recuperation, the Braves were selected for a role in the Southern
[Fra]nce invasion — and their beloved Brig. Gen. Frederick was reassigned
[to] command the assault's Airborne. Their target in DRAGOON was the Lles
[d'H]yeres, on the left end of the Riviera landings. This was a difficult mission,
[giv]en the looming cliffs where beaches would have been nice, backed by
[roll]ing and craggy terrain dominated by bombproof forts from the Napoleonic
[er]a and pillboxes.

Out of rubber boats and up ropes in darkness, the Force was ashore before
[th]e defenders noticed. Outposts were rooted out one by one, until only two
[for]ts and a fortified chateau held out. Answering a ringing fieldphone in a
[jus]t-overrun position, an NCO had a chat with the commander of the chateau.
[Th]e German was unwilling to capitulate to a mere raid. Arguments to per-
[su]ade him that a serious invasion was on were fruitless. Eschewing diplo-
[m]acy, the attackers stormed the place instead. One fort fell, bazookas
[pu]nching in its antique gates. The other was defiant until the big guns of a
[Ro]yal Navy battleship spoke.

Ceding the isles to the Free French, the Force was attached to Frederick's
[1s]t ABTF for the slow, low-priority advance eastward, replacing the British
[2n]d Independent Parachute Brigade (a grudgingly cooperative helpmate at
[be]st). Teamed with the 509th, 463rd PFAB, 602nd pack howitzer FAB,
[64]2nd Infantry Antitank Company, and 887th Airborne Engineer Aviation
[Co]mpany, it rolled up resistance from Grasse to Monaco to the Italian border.

Before leaving Montana for combat, the 1st Special Service Force tried to take
"mugshots" of all its members. These illustrate examples of oddities in uniform.
Left: a Canadian officer, seconded from the Ontario militia Perth Regiment. He
wears the Force's crossed arrows as his Yank mates would, but at a different
angle. Other than these, the jump wings, and the red, white and blue shoulder
cord, his dress is Canadian. Right: one of the
regimental surgeons, an American, wears the
Medical Department caduceus superimposed on
the crossed arrows, with a pre-war gabardine
blouse and crossbelt. (1st Special Service Force
Association)

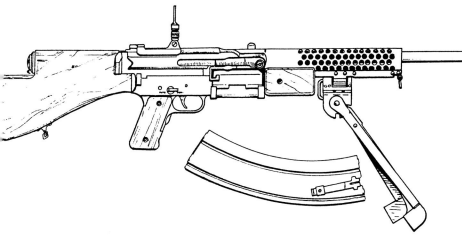

The Johnson M1941 light machine gun had many advanced features
and anticipated the "assault rifles" of later decades. Three thousand
of them, ordered by the Dutch East Indies government, passed to the
Marine Corps, which issued them to Parachute and Raider units. The
1st Special Service Force of the Army liked them enough to trade two
tons of plastic explosive for 125 of them. Its distinctive 20-round single-
row magazine was inserted from the left side and could be reloaded
with loose rounds or Springfield five-round stripper clips via the gate
on the right side. It was five pounds lighter than the BAR and had an
adjustable cyclic rate (300 to 900 rpm), plus a barrel easily dismounted.

Identified only as the "3rd Platoon," Braves of the 1st Special Service Force at Cassano, Italy, November 1943. (Robert Durkee)

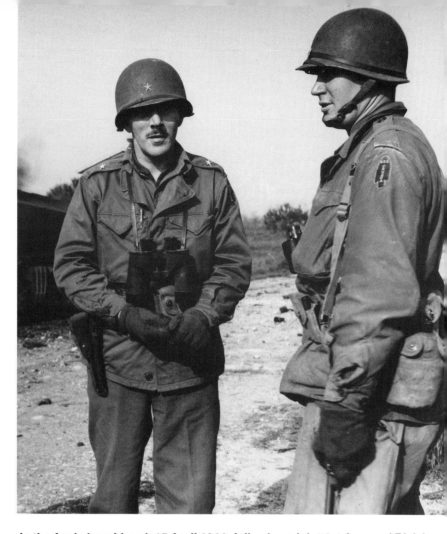

In the Anzio beachhead, 15 April 1944, following a joint 1st Armored Division-Special Service Force raid on Cerro Alto and Litoranea, the commander of the Force, Brig. Gen. Robert T. Frederick, talks things over with Lt. Col. Robert Moore, leader of the Force's 2nd Regiment. The smoldering Sherman tank behind them came to grief on a mine. Both officers wear the green M1943 field jacket, then very new. Quartermaster reports of the ongoing troop test of the M1943 family of gear dwell on the 3rd Infantry Division and make no mention of the Force being issued it. (U.S. Army)

The color guard of the Force and three recipients of the Silver Star for action in the Anzio pocket, 14 March 1944. The inclusion of the British Union Jack denotes the unique U.S.-Canadian makeup of the Force. (U.S. Army)

the road to Rome: Black Devils of the Force share a joke with a group of German prisoners, 2 June 1944. The diagonal zipper on the hip of the center "Brave" clearly distinguishes his trousers as the Mountain type. The 1st SSF usually wore these with jump boots, but this soldier appears to be wearing Italian mountaineering boots! (U.S. Army)

Barneville, France, probably October 1944. The new commander of the 1st SSF, Col. Edwin A. Walker, stands by during a briefing. Although most men here wear the fur-trimmed ski parka that had long been customary with the unit, a few wear the later Parka Overcoat. The man at left front uses a German tornister pack. (1st Special Service Force Association)

The first "Menton Day," December 1944: When the 1st SSF broke up, its 620 surviving Canadians left for new assignments in Canadian units. Here, 44 officers gather for a souvenir photo at Villenueve-Loubet. Seven of them went to the 1st Canadian Para Bn in the British 6th Airborne-Division; 37 went to non-Airborne units in Italy. (Bill Story)

35

Tourists of the Force: In the leisurely days of early 1945 when the 1st SSF was remaking itself at the 474th Infantry Regiment, American Red Cross representative Getty Page, Capt. (Chaplain) Robert G. Essig, and Lewis J. Merrim visited now-quiet battlefields in northern France. (Robert Durkee)

The 1st Special Service Force was the first — but not the only — unit to wear the reversible parka. The first variant — with no button fly at the throat and fur around the cuffs — is at the right.

After weeks of artillery duels and patrolling, 5 December saw inactivation at the coastal town of Menton. Like other odds and ends elite units, the 1st Special Service Force was done in by the changed character of the war in Europe. With Army Groups locked in final battle, a non-standard, mixed-nationality outfit of "Indian warfare" experts were not invited. Though a lineal connection is not official, U.S. Forcemen largely went into the new 474th Infantry Regiment that soldiered on as rear area security troops before becoming the American contingent in Norway. Selected parachute-qualified men went to the Airborne Divisions. Many Canadians passed into the 1st Canadian Division in Italy, while others headed north to new units, including the 1st Can Para Bn of the British 6th Airborne Division. By then a two-star, Frederick took command of the veteran 45th "Thunderbird" Infantry Division.

To reflect its bi-national identity, insignia of Indian motif were adopted. The officer and enlisted crossed arrows were previously authorized the U.S. Indian Scouts. Canadian regs required "CANADA" to be prominently displayed, so Northerner Other Ranks wore the disc shown in place of "U.S." on appropriate garments.

DRAGOON: THE CHAMPAGNE CAMPAIGN

An invasion of Southern France had been discussed by the Allies even before they had elected to climb the "soft underbelly" route up the Italian boot. Later, it was seen as a gambit to precede the Normandy landings, to siphon off evermore Wehrmacht strength southward. The slow slog in Italy and the increasingly ravenous appetite of OVERLORD shelved the idea — until Eisenhower revived it, insisting on a second line of advance into Germany. To implement this Operation DRAGOON, a force including an Airborne Division was hypothesized.

But WHAT Airborne Division?! There was no such thing in the Mediterranean theater! The British had their 2nd Independent Parachute Brigade Group, but the Yanks were limited to the well-worn 509th Parachute Infantry Battalion and the incomplete 463rd Parachute Field Artillery Battalion born at Anzio. In April and May 1944, however, three more units of import hove into the region: the 517th Parachute Regimental Combat Team, the 550th Glider Infantry Battalion, and the 1st (and only) Battalion, 551st PIR.

Through June and July, these units (and others, with no previous Airborne connections) were stitched together into an ad hoc thing dubbed the Seventh Army Airborne Division (Provisional), commanded by Brig Gen. Robert T. Frederick (late of the 1st Special Service Force). A more dignified and permanent-sounding successor outfit called the 1st Airborne Task Force was

Chet Kochersperger (armed with a liberated Polish Radom pistol) does the honors for Pvt. Hatten, Ciampino airfield. (Mrs. Chester Kochersperger)

After its arrival in the war zone, the 517th RCT received its baptism of fire while attached to the 36th Infantry Division around Grosseto. Here a patrol of the 596th Parachute Engineer Company forms up before sallying forth. (Dr. Charles E. Pugh)

An instance of spray-painted camo in two tones, probably black and olive drab. "Doc" Lechleiter assists trooper Mildenstein of Company A, 517th PIR. (Mrs. Chester Kochersperger)

Two views of Medical Department-produced aidman's accoutrements: The bag could be worn singly, hanging from their own narrow strap, or in pairs suspende from the specialized canvas-yoke harness shown or the pistol belt. The full r included a short connecting strap worn across the front between bags. Thes figures show the two canteens medics routinely carried, Geneva Cross helm markings and brassard, sidearm "for personal defense," and the standard fir aid pouch.

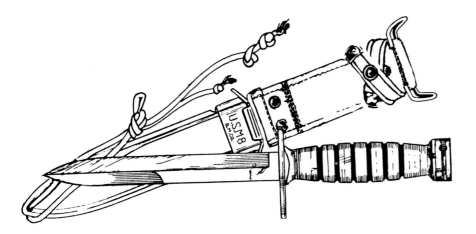

The M-4 knife-bayonet was an adaptation of the knife-only M-3 trench knife f 1943, equipped with a muzzle ring on the crossguard and catch at the butt f mounting on the carbine (itself modified with a new forearm band with bayon stud). The M-4 was adopted in late 1943 and followed the M-3 on production lin by the turn of the year. The M-8 plastic scabbard was born in February 194 and 100,000 were manufactured that year. The addition of the belt-hook resulte in the M-8A1 variant.

August, D-1: Lt. Col. Richard J. Seitz, commanding 2nd Battalion of the 517th ...cond from left, rear) and the enlisted men of his DRAGOON stick. No one here ...ars "paratrooper uniform," instead making do with OD woolies and HBT fa-...ues. (Lt. Gen. Richard J. Seitz)

Dick Young, "Big Lew" Lewis, Fred Canziani, Campion, and Salinas. (Fred Canziani)

...nstituted at War Department order on 16 July and officially activated five ...ys later. Its staff was assembled from disparate sources, including the Air-...rne units fresh from home and a shipment of talent from the 13th Airborne ...vision back Stateside. With the newly concocted Provisional Troop Carrier ...Division of the USAAF, they worked hard to meld the odds and ends into ...riable unit. While the 517th was encouraged to get a taste of frontline ex-...rience with the 36th Infantry Division above Rome, the untried units and ...ver-Airborne elements were run through the Airborne Training Center at ...apani in westernmost Sicily. The "instant Airborne" included the recently ...tivated 512th Airborne Signal Company, the 887th Airborne Aviation En-...eer Company on loan from the USAAF, the 334th Quartermaster Com-...ny, and the 676th Medical Company. Fire-support add-ons comprised the ...2nd Field Artillery Battalion, the Anti-Tank Company from the famed ...panese-American 442nd RCT, and two companies from Chemical Mortar ...ttalions (A/2 and D/83).

The concept of the DRAGOON Airborne mission (codenamed RUGBY) ...lled for preventing the enemy from moving their sparse mobile reserves ...where they could make trouble for the main landings between St. Tropez ...d Nice. This scheme, and the growing possibility that the enemy would ...oose to flee deeper inland rather than face a no-win engagement, made

DRAGOON, 15 August 1944: Paratroopers (probably from 1st Battalion, 551st PIR, as only that unit embarked in daylight) take their ease. Two men carry rifle grenades in packing tubes strapped to their musettes, and one has already equipped himself with a German pistol. (George Rosie)

The designers of the Waco CG-4 glider envisioned it landing in relatively seda fashion on airstrips or meadows clear of obstructions — not bulldozing throu hedgerows, fences, and earthworks. To reinforce the front and reduce dama to the crew, the Griswold Nose was devised. Unfortunately, it proved tardy reaching the war. Only a few were used in OVERLORD, and though availal for 40 percent of the craft in DRAGOON, there was no time for installation. significant number did make VARSITY. An equivalent "cow-catcher" was work into the structure of the CG-15.

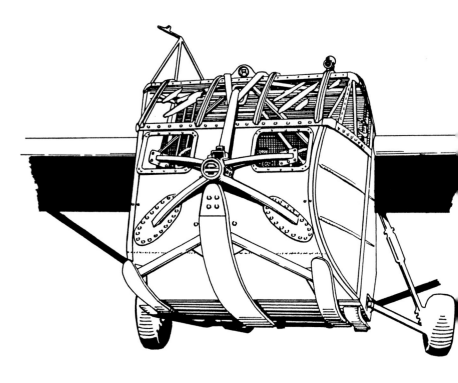

Glidermen, 15 August. Though not identified, these may be members of the 51: Airborne Signal Company, formed for DRAGOON with jumpers drawn from 82nd and 101st and glidermen pulled out of replacement depots. The 512th w later used to form the First Airborne Army's 112th Airborne Signal Battalion a was resurrected in 1986 as part of the 1st Special Operations Command.

M-1 and M-1A1 models of the venerable Thompson were devised by Savage ns. Engaged by the government as an alternate source of the M1928A1 in 1942, age production line technicians were expert enough to see through the need- s complications of Auto-Ordnance's 20-year-old design and recommend nges. After a proprietary wrangle with Auto-Ordnance (which was later charged profiteering), the compensator, barrel cooling fins, detachable stock, adjust- rear sight, and breech-locking mechanism were eliminated. Shortly after M-1 entered production, it was further simplified (as the M-1A1) with a fixed g pin. The "Holster Assembly" is an Air Forces item; each Troop Carrier 7 was authorized a Thompson — to ward off enemy aircraft and for self- tection at remote landing sites.

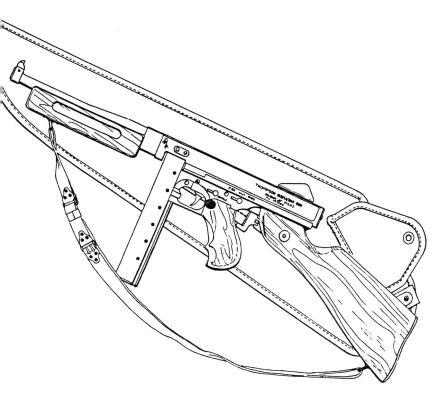

Unidentified glidermen move off the La Motte LZ. Their gear suggests they are headquarters or service troops rather than infantrymen. (U.S. Army)

op Carrier records tell of one jumper of the 460th PFAB who somehow failed nake the initial drop, but was then voluntarily recycled to hit the silk during D + 1 resupply mission. Though uncertain, the unamused paratrooper here be that singleton. The odd scabbard for his Thompson is an item of Air Forces e.

The commander of the 1st Airborne Task Force, Maj. Gen. Robert T. Frederick takes part in the ceremonies marking the liberation at the Le Muy townhall on D + 2. The mayor (right) was an active maquisard. Frederick had received one-star rank in January, then received two stars in June with the Task Force job. (U.S. Army)

Between objectives, a 509th trooper considers his next move. (U.S. Arm

quick control of the road nets the 1st ATF's first order of business. Parach units, minus the 1/551, would lead the way, dropping between 0330 and 05 hours on 15 August. Starting at 0800, the first glider lift would bring in British artillery. The major glider landings would be deferred until dusk, t cause of the great numbers of obstructions and mines known to be on t LZ's. According to the scenario, what hadn't been cleared by the early ju ers would be dealt with by the 1/551 just prior to the landing.

As with OVERLORD, a lot depended on the Pathfinders. Six Americ teams (one from each jumping battalion and even one for the non-jumpi 550th, according to records) trained hard, taking every possible precauti to ensure success. But bad drops undid them. This time it was a heavy bla ket of fog and some cranky radar aids that sent the airplanes roaming arou in the blackness. The 509/551/550 serials were dumped 10 to 15 miles they made no contributions in their specialty. The 517th teams came to ea a mere three miles astray, but were so puzzled by the rough terrain and p

en of the 509th Parachute Infantry Battalion demolition section, probably D-1
Follonica airbase. (509th Association)

Paratrooping photogs Ssgt. Ed Peterson and Sgt. Irving Liebowitz discuss professional matters in Le Muy, 17 August. (U.S. Army)

up they had to wait for daylight to figure out where they were. Thereupon
ey jumped it for DZ "A," with Germans harassing them, in time to assist
e later drops. By some quirk, the British teams were inserted in fine fettle.
filtrated OSS teams tried to set up EUREKA beacons with the help of the
aquis, but these had no known effect.

As it developed, when the main drop arrived with 396 planeloads of para-
oopers, the lack of slick Pathfinding did not matter. The fog was so thick
at aircrews could not have trusted any ground signals received. Careful
avigating brought the sticks in roughly on target. The troops' memories of
rrain briefings saved the day, as they recognized hilltops poking through
e mists. Half of the 509/463 team landed close to the mark. The other half
ent out too early, so came to earth 10 miles away. This proved a good deal,
s their impromptu *pied-a-terre* was the resort town of St. Tropez. There they
efriended the *Maquis* and, with pieces of the 3rd Infantry Division moving
o from the beaches, cleaned out the town's citadel. The rest of the 509/463
nder Lt. Col. William Yarborough was mopping up around Le Mitan with
e British cousins.

The 517th RCT drops around Le Muy were scattered and varied in effec-
veness. The 3rd Battalion fared worst, blindly deposited in three clumps 15
25 miles wrong. Nevertheless, by noon the "Battling Buzzards" of Col.
*upert Graves' RCT managed to take nearly all assigned objectives. Though
t. Col. Mel Zais' 3/517 was frantically trying to catch up with the war,
*aj. William Boyle's 1/517 was pummeling some recalcitrant *Deutscher*

soldaten at Les Arcs. La Motte fell to the 2nd Battalion, Lt. Col. Richard Seitz's
outfit, and Lt. Col. Raymond Cato's 460th PFAB had little difficulty in getting
most of its guns into action.

Airborne landings resumed at 1745 hours. The Horsas that had aborted
the morning mission (when only Wacos completed the trip) came in first, cart-
ing more gunners. Next came the second paratroop lift, flawlessly putting
all 736 men of the 551st on the zone. German flak was sparse. As Lt. Col.
Wood Joerg's "Goya" parachutists assembled, over 330 Wacos came into
view. These carried the 550th and sundry support units. Though the fly-in
was fine, parking was a disaster. Only some of the "Rommel asparagus"
poles had been cleared — French helpers had been put to work on the wrong
fields. First arrivals skillfully set down between them, playing a dodge-em game
that sheared a lot of wings. But openings dwindled for latecomers. The con-
gested scene was enough to make some fliers go on to find unprogrammed
fields elsewhere.

43

"Go for Broke" tank-killers of the 442nd Infantry's gliderborne contingent demonstrate how to engage targets of opportunity. (John Alicki)

Glider assault wings made on the Riviera for AT crews of the 442nd Infantry Regiment, the design incised into sterling silver.

Men of the 463rd PFAB stroll through Ste. Maxime on D + 1. The 463rd was formed overseas, in the Anzio beachhead, with a personnel transfusion from the 456th PFAB of the 82nd Airborne Division. At Anzio, shared experiences with the 1st SSF caused it to be fondly deputized by the "Braves" as "Force Arty." For the "Champagne Campaign" it was paired with the 509th PIB; it was eventually assigned to the 101st Airborne Division in March 1945.

nbat Engineers: 596th Parachute Engineer npany commander Cpt. Robert Dalrymple and erne Moore reconoiter the road to Luceram 'Firing Point No. 45,'' September 1944. (Dr. rles E. Pugh)

Welsh of Headquarters Company, 1/551st iouthern France. His helmet is emblazoned ι the unit's palm tree emblem. (Jim Welsh)

With the Airborne landings a great success overall, momentum was kept with the capture of Le Muy on D + 1 by an assortment of units and guer- s. Some of the *Maquis* bit off more than they could chew in Draguinan, the *Amis* came to their rescue. This venture netted the 1/551 scads of oners, including the headman and staff of the opposing German LXII corps. 517th settled accounts at Les Arcs as its 3rd Battalion came trekking The wanderers' respite was brief and they wearily got on with tidying up valley leading to Les Arcs that evening.

By D + 3, the situation was under control. In the crucial early stages of invasion, the Airborne had seen to it that no reinforcements reached the enders. Seventh Army felt confident enough to make a bold decision for uick pursuit in the Rhone valley, not to let the Boche slip away. While this olded, the Airborne inherited the eastern flank, where German and Fas- Italian armies still lurked.

The liberation of metropolitan Cannes and Nice was nice, memorable for embraceable *femmes* and free-flowing bubbly. But the spoil-sport Krauts did not always decamp graciously and serious engagements still took place. Push- ing on and leaving the rear echelon types ensconced in the tourist area, the combat units overran Grasse and seeped into the high country of the Mari- time Alps. There they settled in to outpost the uneasy frontier facing Italy. While the eyes of the world shifted to more exciting news, the Task Force alternated alpine skirmishes with junkets for morale repairs in the rear. Through the autumn, artillery raids and aggressive patrols were standard fare. Finally Frederick's command was relieved, beginning in late October.

Pushing hard on the Wehrmacht: Povinelli, Westerman, Stevens and Tilton. Note the wrapping of mattress ticking on the machine gun, to allow holding the hot barrel in assault fire. (Fred Canziani)

Camping in the clear mountain air: Starr, MacDade and Canziani. (Fred Canzi▶

After a proper Thanksgiving observance, the ATF was broken up. (Though not widely known, the 1st Airborne Task Force's history lived on, its lineage continued by consolidation with Brereton's First Airborne Army.) Its subordinate units entrained on the "40 and 8" railcars that hauled an earlier generation of expeditionary Yanks. Through miserable weather, the trains snaked northward to Soissons. The 550th split off and headed for England and attachment to the 17th Airborne Division. The 512th Signal was first passed to Ridgway's Corps, then absorbed in the creation of the 112th Airborne Signal Battalion for Brereton's Army, which had been activated on 2 August. No less than kindred spirits in the 82nd and the 101st, the DRAGOON veterans turned their attentions to liberty in Paris.

The "Bazooka" was a 2.36-inch bore launcher that fired revolutionary-shaped charge armor-piercing rockets. It was not greatly respected by users — its short range made it necessary to get close to tanks, accuracy was unpredictable, and it had little chance against Panthers, let alone Tigers. The M-1 model was introduced in North Africa. The improved M-9 entered service with high-priority units by mid-1944, and the first break-down two-piece M-9A1 (here) reached jump units after Normandy. Four rockets, packed in cardboard tubes, were carried in the bag shown.

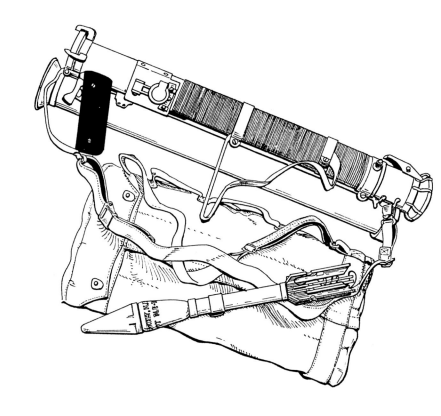

Some of the pilots of the 1st Airborne Task Force at Grasse, August 1944. (Col. George F. Morris)

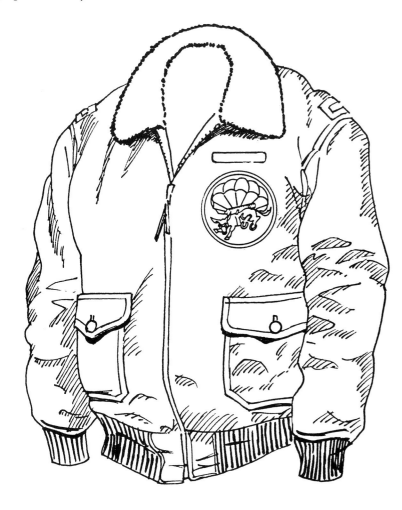

The olive green cloth B-10 flight jacket was expected to replace the less practical — but tonsorially classic — A-2 horsehide type. The emblem is that of the 460th Parachute Field Artillery Battalion, 517th Parachute RCT.

The boys of the 460th PFAB at Nice in October 1944. Lt. Larry Overton displays the 460th's patch on his B-10 flight jacket. (Col. George F. Morris)

47

MARKET-GARDEN: BLOOD, SWEAT, AND TEARS

When German armies were snagged by the Anglo-American thresher in mid-1944, the strategic complexion of the war changed. Suddenly a gradual roll-up on a broad front was out, and "End the War in '44" fever was in. With logistics the make-or-break factor, Eisenhower turned down Omar Bradley's call for a drive on the center. Instead, Ike gave the nod to Field Marshal Montgomery's rival proposal. In the bargain, Monty agreed to use the Airborne in its first strategic outing, Operation MARKET-GARDEN.

This combined armored-airborne pincers move thrust deep into Holland and had the goals of turning the northern flank of the Siegfried Line and cutting off the hordes of Germans along the coast guarding the approaches to the prized port of Amsterdam. As the infant First Allied Airborne Army brainstormed plans, British tankers raced through Belgium. With the enemy seeming to collapse, optimism soared. The cheery mind-set of course had dire consequences, most especially for the poorly-led British Airborne troops. On the opposing side, the generals were neither foolish nor sleeping. The vulnerability of Holland did not escape them — unnoticed by the Allies, they were regrouping.

The ground-bound GARDEN phase was promised the cushion of "an Airborne carpet" to ease the progress of its "one-tank front" up the single narrow road. The welcome mat at the southern end would be the U.S. 101st Airborne Division, laid down between the city of Eindhoven and the town of Uden. The next scatter-rug would be the 82nd Airborne Division, centering on Grave and Nijmegen. The topmost, deepest patch was to be the British 1st Airborne Division, just across the all-important Rhine. A multiplicity of

Enlisted personnel of the J-4 logistics staff, 1st Allied Airborne Army, early S[e]ptember 1944: (standing) Pte. Clayton, SSgt. Wasserman, Pte. Lofty, SSgt. Bro[w] T-5 Griffin, TSgt. Steinberg, Sgt. LaValle; (front row) SSgt. Thomas, Pvt. C[on]nie, SSgt. Givens, Capt. Ryan, and Sgt. Johnson. (Herbert L. Schumacher)

Cottesmore airdrome, 16 September 1944: A good shot of how wheeled loads were put into Waco gliders. These jeeps of the 407th Airborne Quartermaster Company and 782nd Airborne Ordnance Company, 82nd Airborne Division, went to LZ T and landed in more or less good order. (U.S. Army)

bridges interrupted what was to become known as "Hell's Highway." As j[o] as the advertisements from higher headquarters described it, it occurred few of the participants that these problems would make Arnhem one brid[ge] too far.

MARKET was a daytime operation, kicked off on Sunday, 17 Septemb[er] 1944. Even more than with OVERLORD, tactical air support was out ahe[ad] of the fleet of 1,545 transports and 478 gliders. Pathfinders encountered major hangups. On the southern approach route, the Screaming Eagles' weathered the first flak.

The main part of the 101st landed above Eindhoven. The first of ma[ny] bridges fell to 1/502, but the town of Best was too tough a nut to pass to t[he] rest of Col. Michaelis' 502nd PIR. The 506th had the most serious setba[ck] of the day, fighting through to the bridge at Zon only in time to see it blo[wn] up. All in all, the 101st did well, with regrets only for not having seized Ei[nd] hoven itself — and that the British armor had not shown up as promise[d].

In the 82nd's swatch of carpet, drops were accurate and uneventful. T[he] 504th PIR alit at either end of the major bridge at Grave and claimed it for [it] with. To the east, the 505th secured Groesbeek and kept moving to take defensive positions on the wooded hills of the Reichswald, beyond which [lay] Deutschland. After muddling through flak and severe ground fire, the 50[8th]

R split up. The 1st Battalion sent patrols into Nijmegen, to size up its very ge bridge. As the battle developed, Nijmegen grew into a fierce battleground. ough good luck allowed the early destruction of the controls for emplaced molitions, stymying German plans to drop the mighty span into the Waal, e foe kept it through three days of heavy fighting.

Glider landings of the first day brought in 46 of 50 Wacos sent to the All-mericans, with the major contents a battery of the 80th Airborne AAA/AT attalion to lend a hand to the 376th PFAB that had jumped with the 505th. e 101st scheduled more gliders (53 of 70 making it), but these carried neither illery nor infantry. Pointing up the Screaming Eagles' trust in close air sup-rt and the reach of British guns accompanying the GARDEN advance, the 1st opted for reconnaissance gunjeeps, medics, commo and HQ assets. e third wave of gliders delivered the British 1st Airborne staff (including aj. Gen. Urquhart) to Arnhem, using 35 Wacos and Horsas.

The morrow brought some welcome reinforcements, despite worsening eather. With the 101st, the 506th PIR took Eindhoven to greet the lanquid Brit-s, while the 501st beat off desultory probes. Still at Best, the 502nd struggled th a superior force. Finally the afternoon came, with the lift of two glider in-ntry units — 2/327 and 1/401 — to add to the 502nd's project. The 428 Wacos so hauled more support troops, mostly engineers and medics.

D + 1 dawned promisingly for the 82nd, but took a turn for the worse. Ger-ans surged down the highway and out of the forest, forcing parts of the)8th and 505th back and overrunning what was scheduled to be the day's Z. Fortunately, these adversaries were not first-class units, but scraped-up ampfgruppen. While the weather forestalled the glider arrival anyhow, the oopers (including two companies of the 307th Airborne Engineer Battalion xercising their secondary role as infantrymen) enforced eviction. That ac-omplished, 385 gliders dropped in, disgorging three GFAB's and another

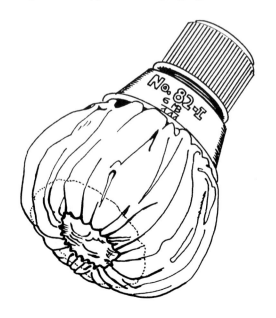

Last-minute issue of controlled materiel, Cottesmore. Other than styrettes of the narcotic painkiller morphine, goodies comprise sticks of Composition C-2 plastic explosive and No. 82 Gammon grenades. Here the placement of the No. 8 special detonator in the primer cup of this British device is being discussed. The trooper at left holds a grenade, empty of plastique and with its elasticized "sack" peeled back. (U.S. Army)

This jeep of the 407th QM is rigged with a .50 caliber machine gun and pintle mount, items usually associated with front-line reconnaissance units.

AT battery. With flak by then zeroed in and eager for targets, some serials landed off the LZ, with dozens of them in enemy territory and a few even inside the Reich. Many of the newly arriving cannoneers huddled together to hold off assailants and work their way to friendly lines that night, minus their howitzers.

The next act in the air show was the innovative resupply run by B-24 bombers. This had its major accomplishment in proving that high-altitude bombardment people do not adapt well to low-level troop carrier work. In a staff snafu, the two Wings were each given the other's target data. Only as the Liberators were warming up was the error rectified. Misreading the signals and dumping their loads prematurely, or not releasing the first time and doing a 180 turn to fly back through the trailing serials, then violating good sense by naively turning for home in wide, climbing arcs — casually baring their bellies to drooling predators peering through the sights of flak guns below — did wonders. For the 82nd recovery of these expensive bundles ran 80 percent, but only less than half could be found by the 101st.

The weather was even less kind on D + 2. Overnight, the 101st had thoug better of the situation and repacked its next flock of gliders with artillery a more dogfaces. The skies were so inhospitable,. however, 120 Wacos we deducted from the mission before they reached Dutch airspace. Flying und the glowering clouds attracted more ground fire, and just 209 of 382 CG-4A dispatched got through. The unit hit worst was the 907th GFAB, getting ju two dozen men and none of its pack 105's in. But the 377th PFAB (cond scending to ride in gliders) managed to insert a dozen 75's, ready to go ju in time to dislocate an armored attack. No new units reached the 82nd th day, as the 325th GIR was fogged in back in Old Blighty, and the only a op for it was a resupply drop. Gavin, with only 2/505 and some British arm to work with, made a fresh move on the Nijmegen bridge. Repeated attemp yielded only blood.

A lieutenant of the 82nd checks a silk survival map with his stick. His should patch is a British-made felt version. One soldier wears the first aid packet tie to his cartridge belt, another on the handle of his entrenching tool. (U.S. Arm

buckled combat boot was first issued for test in Tunisia, the prototypes being
inary field shoes with leather "gaiters" added. A few trickled down to vari-
s units in the Mediterranean and northern France before the 82nd and 101st
re issued them in August-September 1944.

On 20 September, the fortunes of the two American Airborne forces varied.
e Screaming Eagles broke up attacks by some *panzergrenadiers* and a
scellany of Luftwaffe *ersatz* soldiers. The 82nd was hard-pressed, primar-
by a major venture by hard-core *fallschirmjager* units, for which the 505th
gaged the services of 185 "midnight gamblers" of the glider pilot gang.
. Reuben Tucker's 504th PIR, on the fringes thusfar, was dealt into the
ne at the Nijmegen bridge. Its unenviable task was to get across the river
canvas and plywood "assault" boats in a flanking move. The 3/504 led
way. Heavy supporting fires from cannon and aircraft, simultaneous fron-
attacks by the 2/505 and tanks, as well as a smokescreen (that perversely
fted) did not foreclose a duckshoot for the Nazis. But the heroic paddlers
o gained the opposite bank rose up to crush the defenders, and from the
th end of the span witnessed the tanks put an end to the episode. The
dge was taken.

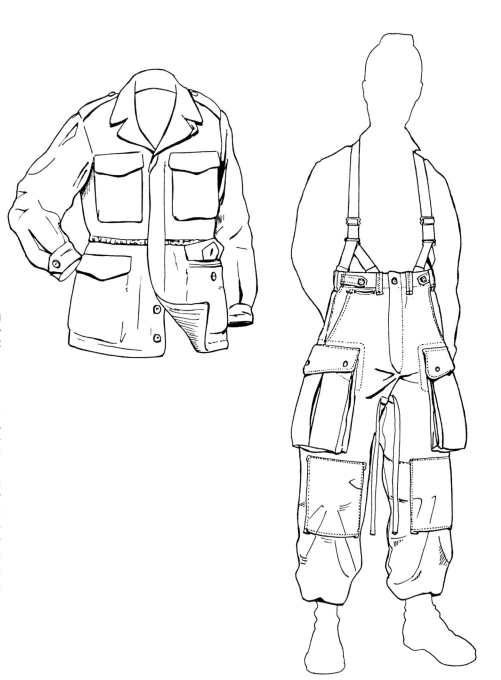

The M1943 field trousers were modified in the ETO to paratroopers' tastes: cargo
pockets copied from the M1942 jump trousers, leg tie-tapes, and knee reinforcements. Fabric for these often came from old uniforms or salvaged canvas.

82nd commanding general Maj. Gen. James M. Gavin confers with his primary staff officers and regimental commanders before the MARKET-GARDEN departure. Left to right: Lt. Col. Walter Winton, G-2; Col. William Ekman (sitting), 505th PIR; Col. Reuben H. Tucker (in leather jacket), 504th PIR; Lt. Col. Al Ireland (partly covered), G-1; Col. Frank March, Divarty; Lt. Col. Robert Wienecke (sitting), Chief of Staff; Lt. Col. Al Marin, G-4; Gavin; Col. Charles Billingslea, 325th GIR; and Col. John Norton, G-3. (U.S. Army)

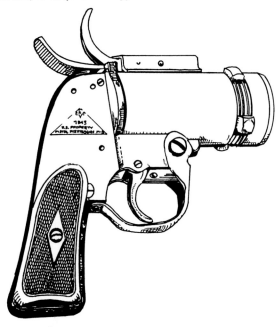

The M-8 37mm pyrotechnic pistol used in all services for signalling.

Capt. Arie Bestebreurtje, the 82nd's liaison with the Dutch underground, a Hugo Olson, General Gavin's aide. "Harry" wears a green Commando beret wi Dutch lion badge, blue and red COMMANDO shoulder titles, British jump wir on his chest (signifying a completed SOE mission), and the Special Forces wir on his sleeve. Also note the Dutch rank stars on his collars, Sykes-Fairbairn d ger, and American jump boots. After the war, he became an American citiz and a clergyman; he drowned tragically in an ice-skating mishap in Decem 1982. (Arie Bestebreurtje estate via Ron Fischer)

A glider pilot (ranking as a Flight Officer) shod in unoiled combat boots poses with a quartet of Battery A, 319th GFAB gunners at Barkston Heath airfield. The lieutenant wears green Combat Leader tabs (then a very recent innovation) on his shoulder straps and a USAAF-style leather nametape. The center man has "Dick Evans" embroidered over his pocket. The Glider Assault wings at left mark a veteran of the Normandy landings. (Robert Anderson)

en of Company E, 505th PIR prior to boarding for MARKET: (front) Cal (last ame unknown), Jimmy Keenan, Sgt. Wheeler; (rear) Gal Taylor, Lt. Phillips, John uffard. (Tony DeMayo)

A group of 501st men huddle before embarkation. In the center, what may be the jumpmaster wears a sheepskin flight jacket under his field jacket.

Troopers of the 501st check each other's harness. Here the white webbing used to convert the harnesses to the British quick-release closure (QRC) shows well. Shoulder patches were obscured by a wartime censor. (101st Airborne Division Association via George Rosie)

The same stick piles in, this time their patches unscathed. Note the green canvas extensions on the tan Griswold bags. (U.S. Army)

Poor weather on D + 3 precluded glider missions to the Yank throwrugs, but resupply sorties were flown — into a storm of shot and shell. By now diligent in evasive action, the transports were furtive enough to get only 60 percent of the bundles for the 82nd, and 30 percent for the 101st, on target. An added attraction was the troop jump on the last battery of the 377th PFAB, through the maelstrom of flak.

On D + 4, the 504th defeated a counterattack of the Nijmegen bridge, but the day was much the same. With the fizzling of the British road dash, the grim fate of the Red Berets at Arnhem became obvious. Though too little, too late, the Polish 1st Parachute Brigade that had been weathered-in did finally get elements aloft and got about a thousand jumpers in; some Polish soldiers were so keen to kill Nazis that they swam the Rhine to get into the shrinking perimeter at Arnhem.

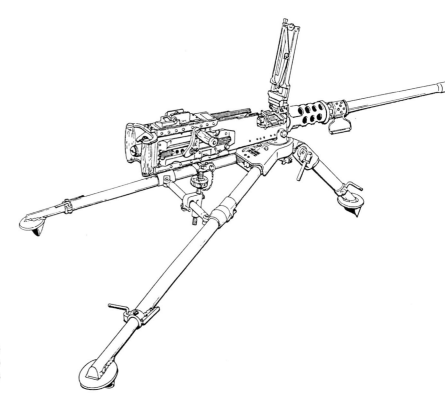

The M-2 Browning .50 caliber machine gun was not usually found with Airborne infantry, but rather in the artillery and support units, where there were jeeps to carry it and feed its appetite for ammunition. It was useful in beating off attacks that penetrated as far as the gun pits or trains.

On the ground in Holland, a 505th jeep patrol chats up the crew of British Sherman tank — which has a dead man rolled up in canvas on its rear deck.

ssing the time in Groesbeek are two paras (likely of the 505th or 508th PIR) aring odd adaptations of the winter combat overalls usually associated with nored vehicle crews — these have cargo pockets from M1942 jump suits added. e man at right seems to have a unit marking on his helmet.

There were no drops at all on the 22nd, the day the 101st piled on in a e-for-all bout for possession of Veghel. The Germans struck there just as Screaming Eagles wre shifting units to cover that locale. In turn, the Krauts gled with the 2/501, some transient Limey armor, and the just-arriving 2/506, 01, and 81st AAA/AT tank-killers. Not able to capture the place, Hitler's n next tried to cut the road above and below it. The 327th GIR, its attached 1st GFAB, and 3/501 ended the southern interdiction.

On D + 7, 24 September, Monty owned up to defeat and bade the survi-s at Arnhem to exfiltrate as best they could. Thus parked on the wrong e of the Rhine, the initiative lost, the Allies reshuffled for defense of their mpy salient. The 101st migrated north, above the 82nd, to an area nick-med "The Island." Both divisions settled down to pushing the enclave's ges outward. The Axis forces were by then nicely regrouped and very en-uraged by their successes; the Airborne, especially the 101st, was destined more hard soldiering. Only on D + 57 did the All-Americans come off the e, and their comrades in the 101st set a new record by persisting to D + 71. th then headed for rest camps, where they made the acquaintance of brother opers recently imported through southern France. Together, they got in e mood for a winter of recreation and trips to the wallows of Paris that would doubt disgrace the uniform.

From 24 to 27 September (D + 7 to D + 10), the 101st had its work cut out for it in keeping the road between St. Oedenrode and Veghel open. Here a member of the 326th Airborne Engineer Battalion leads the way for paratroopers, most likely from the 506th PIR, in Veghel. (U.S. Army)

THE BULGE: THE AIRBORNE RESPONDS

Though MARKET-GARDEN had failed, and continued attacks were necessary to keep pressure on Hitler's armies, in late 1944 the Allies felt sure that Germany would soon collapse. The intelligence staffs said the Wehrmacht had no offensive capacity left. Only the weird new V-weapons, the Siegfried Line, and a few months stood between Germany and defeat.

Like all ETO Yanks from Ike on down, Airborne troopers in late autumn turned their attention to making ready for the upcoming climactic spring battles — and for savoring the joys of merrymaking in Paris and lesser French resorts.

But Adolf had once again hatched an unpredicted grand scheme — a plan for a massive counteroffensive. As de Fuhrer saw it, the 1940 surprise attack through the wooded, hilly, "untrafficable" Ardennes would be duplicated, but with the added feature of winter weather. The bold objective dictated to von Rundstedt was the seizure of the major port and transportation hub of Antwerp, to cut off Montgomery's 21st Army Group and hopefully wreck inter-Allied relations.

The panzer armies struck at dawn on 16 December. Through bitter cold and cloaking fog, the rag-tag blitzkrieg cut through the depleted 28th and green 106th Infantry Divisions. Time was of the essence, given such a fragile network. Everything hinged on control of bridges, crossroads, and towns and terrain that dominated them.

In a sideshow effort, the German Airborne made a combat jump on the night of 16-17 December. Led by Col. Baron von der Heydte (a cousin of the man who had tried to blow up Hitler the previous July, Count von Stauffenberg) and cadremen from his veteran 6th Fallschirm Regiment, some 1,200 men were scraped together to drop on the northern shoulder of the salient. It surprised no one that the drop was a flop. Less then one-third of the men had ever made any kind of parachute jump, and only one of the 112 pilots had ever flown a night combat mission, let alone dropped parachutists! The largest group assembled on the ground was less than 300 strong. It could not reach critical terrain or organize for an attack. On the 20th, frustrated survivors broke into three-man teams to exfiltrate. The Baron hobbled into erstwhile-target Monschau and surrendered.

Of greater impact were the other 900 *fallschirmjager,* whose drops — and crashes — were widely dispersed. In this imitation of the Americans' bad drop in Normandy, there was a psywar harvest: G.I. scuttlebutt painted a panicky picture of Nazi parachutists everywhere. Nervousness was redoubled by word of another special unit on the loose: the so-called 150th Panzer Brigade of SS-Obersturmbannfuhrer and commando extraordinaire Otto Skorzeny. This task unit, partially uniformed and equipped as Americans, was to gain control of critical points by infiltration and ruse, and confuse the defenders wherever possible. Gossip had it that the phony G.I.'s were out to kill Eisenhower. One of the sub-plots of The Bulge became impromptu challenges of suspected infiltrators with truth-or-consequences queries like "Who is the Brown Bomber?" and "What's the capital of Wyoming?"

Mere days before The Bulge drastically changed their holiday plans, budd Walter E. Hughes, Al Duhm, and Ed Hahn of Company I, 504th PIR engaged services of a passing sidewalk cameraman to record their suave good looks. Th were dressed up to compete for Christmastime passes to Paris. Duhm inexp ably wears a dark olive USAAF officers' jacket that is an early version of the Jacket Look. (Walter E. Hughes)

e term "Ike jacket" was applied to (from
t to right above) the common-place
Wool Field Jacket"; cut-down Service
cket, Enlisted Men (both in olive drab);
d the Shade 51 officers' private-purchase
riant. Below these are shown for com-
rison two US limited-issue "Field Jack-
,," both made to specifications of the
O Quartermaster — a copy of the
mmy's Battle Dress jacket (with modified
llar) and a wool version of the M1941
eld Jacket.

Eisenhower called out his SHAEF reserves late on the 17th. The XVIII
irborne Corps — in rest camps around Rheims — was to head north pronto.
he order was received by Maj. Gen. Gavin, then acting commander of XVIII
irborne Corps. (Actual commander Lt. Gen. Ridgway and many of his staff-
rs were in England, enjoying some rest, overseeing operational readiness
sts for the newly-arrived 17th Airborne Division and conferring with Gen.
rereton and his First Airborne Army people.)

Before hitting the road for Belgium, Gavin started the ball rolling: the 82nd
ould leave first, at dawn; the 101st by mid-afternoon; the non-divisional out-
ts (recently arrived from southern France) as soon thereafter as possible.
nce there, he determined to send the 82nd to the northern V Corps front,
round Werbomont, and the 101st to VIII Corps, to a road hub town called
astogne.

By this time, Ridgway and company were flying back to Rheims. He alerted
the 17th Airborne Division for priority movement to the front, expecting to
lead an all-Airborne Corps. But bad weather and competing priorities for planes
delayed the Golden Talon and kept it from a major role in the early fights,
and the 82nd and 101st had already parted.

On 20 December, the first U.S. Airborne units came to blows, with the
elite 1st SS Panzer Division. In an action typical of Airborne everywhere in
The Bulge, the 504th PIR of the 82nd threw itself on Kampfgruppe Peiper,
the Nazi vanguard. Its heroic frontal assault into a storm of 20mm flakwagen
fire took the village of Cheneux, but left Company B with just 18 men standing and 41 effectives in Company C. At Trois Ponts, the 505th was glad to
find Yank engineers holding out. They had blown two of the place's namesake
bridges, frustrating Peiper. Hoping to block Peiper from the rear, Company

Unidentified mortarmen of the 82nd celebrate the arrival of Christmas parcels, location undetermined. (82nd Airborne Division Museum)

Basking in a brief thaw in the Belgian winter, troops of the 551st march into S elot on 22 December. (U.S. Army)

E scrabbled across the ruins of one bridge into "Kraut country." When second-wave elements of the Leibstandarte Adolf Hitler rushed to contact, 2/505th commander Lt. Col. Vandervoort was ordered out. Most of Company F was committed to help break contact. The pull-out became a mess, but thinking they had the upper hand, SS panzergrenadiers began wading the river — into the guns of the rest of the Panthers.

The 508th PIR and 325th GIR were on the right flank and in reserve, while non-Airborne units given to Ridgway — the 30th Infantry Division and part of the 3rd Armored Division — tied in on the upper arm of Ridgway's "horse-shoe" line. As the 517th RCT, 509th PIB, and 1/551st PIR arrived, they became the Corps' "wild cards," shuttled back and forth as reinforcements to the "leg" units — deliberately so, as Ridgway felt their fighting spirit would rub off.

A group of 508th troopers in a snowy assembly area, about 20 December. The 82nd's combat elements were trucked non-stop from their restcamps around Rheims to Werbomont, with only whatever clothing and arms they had at hand. Upon detrucking, new overcoats, overshoes, and blankets were doled out. Each man was on his own to contrive some means of carrying the blanket — bootlaces, commo wire, bandoleer straps. (Robert Anderson)

nama, 1943: Field maneuvers for the 1/551st PIR. Joe Cicchinelli (left) and unidentified comrade wear camouflage for the event.

On pass in Brussels, officers of the GOYA's are Lt. Phil Hand, Lt. Quinn, and Capt. Smith. (551st Parachute Infantry Association)

⬤ile training in North Carolina between Panama service and deployment to the O, the 1/551st had the dubious distinction of proving that mass jumps could conducted from gliders in tow. Here they marshal at Laurinburg-Maxton Army Base in the fall of 1943. (Charles Fairlamb)

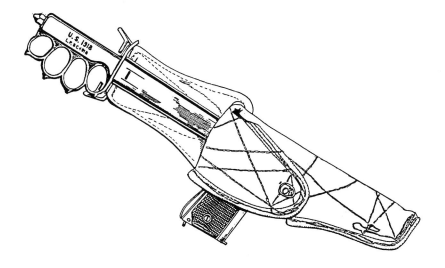

The tropic climate of the Canal Zone engendered this field-expedient canvas holster, made up by riggers of the 1/551st. Its exterior surfaces are painted with tent waterproofing, and it hangs from a leather extender that accommodates the Mark I trench knife. (Edwin F. Schroeder)

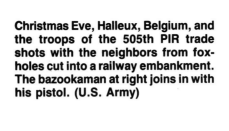

Christmas Eve, Halleux, Belgium, and the troops of the 505th PIR trade shots with the neighbors from foxholes cut into a railway embankment. The bazookaman at right joins in with his pistol. (U.S. Army)

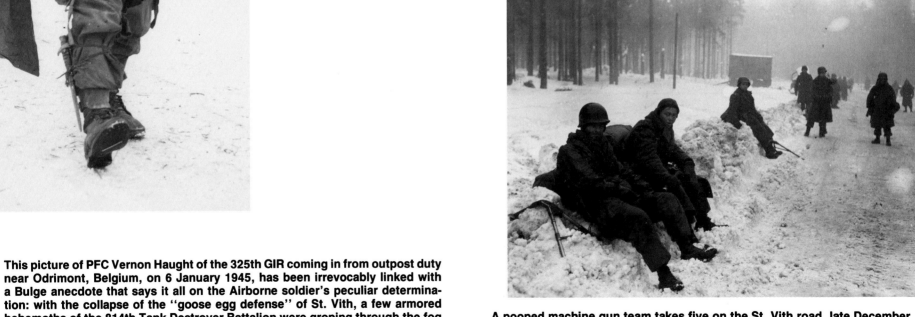

This picture of PFC Vernon Haught of the 325th GIR coming in from outpost duty near Odrimont, Belgium, on 6 January 1945, has been irrevocably linked with a Bulge anecdote that says it all on the Airborne soldier's peculiar determination: with the collapse of the "goose egg defense" of St. Vith, a few armored behemoths of the 814th Tank Destroyer Battalion were groping through the fog trying to find some friendlies. They were challenged by a lone, bedraggled G.I. who asked, "Looking for a safe place? Well, buddy, just pull in behind me — I am the 82nd Airborne and this is as far as those bastards are going!" (U.S. Army)

A pooped machine gun team takes five on the St. Vith road, late December. both the 325th and 504th crisscrossed this area, these troops could be from eit unit. During this period, the 504th "Devils in Baggy Pants" earned their seco Distinguished Unit Citation. (82nd Airborne Division Museum)

Although events in the XVIIIth's sector were crucial to thwarting Hitler's ~~n~~, and the combat thereabouts every bit as fierce, the Screaming Eagles' ~~c~~ stand at Bastogne overshadowed all else in The Bulge. After the 101st ~~k~~ it over (and many odds and ends of armor and artillery units that had ~~ne~~ to rest there), and had "surrounded the poor Germans from the inside," ~~town's~~ critical position became clear. If Kampfgruppe Peiper had done ~~ter~~ in its lunge westward, Bastogne would have been secondary. After first ~~bassing~~ the enclave, then trying to compress it, with the onset of snow on ~~22nd,~~ the enemy tried to get acting commander Brig. Gen. Anthony McAu-~~e~~ to surrender. Befuddled by his legendary response "Nuts!" they had no ~~bice~~ but to turn about and eliminate this obstacle — or perish in the attempt.

The next crisis was the similar situation at St. Vith. There the 7th Armored ~~rision~~ and assorted smaller units held on — more or less surrounded — ~~:il~~ even Ridgway concluded that pulling back was inevitable. On 23 De-~~nber,~~ the 508th PIR shifted to cover their withdrawal, making the acquain-~~ce~~ of the 9th SS Panzer Division in the process.

A new version of a familiar weapon, the M1919A6 light machine gun in service with the 325th GIR. SSgt. Charles Marible and PFC Louis Jenkins look for targets near Odrimont, Belgium, 6 January 1945. (U.S. Army)

~~r~~ the regimental command post, winter warriors of the 517th shape up for ~~atrol.~~ Their armament includes a BAR. (John Alicki)

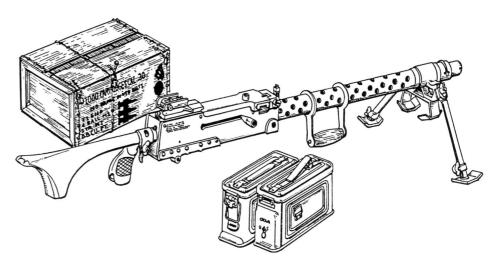

The M1919A5 version of the light machine gun began entering service in the ETO in late 1944. It differed from the M1919A4 in that it had a lightened barrel, carrying handle, sheet-metal buttstock, bipod, and muzzle recoil booster.

Foot soldiers of the 513th move up through the snowscape of Houffalize.

A guncrew of the 155th Airborne AAA/AT Battalion — and riders from the 513 PIR — 17th Airborne Division at Houffalize, 21 January 1945. (U.S. Army)

A patrol of the 509th Parachute Infantry Battalion moves up with the 7th Armored Division near St. Vith, late January. This was the same trailblazing unit that made the first combat jumps in North Africa and accumulated five assault landing credits in the Mediterranean. Before The Bulge, the planned disbandment of the 509th would have reassigned its men to the 101st Airborne Division. But fate intervened to append the outfit to the infantry-poor 3rd and 7th Armored Divisions. When the shooting was over, just seven officers and 48 enlisted men were left standing in the O-Nine. (U.S. Army)

Elsewhere, two German divisions were curling back, into the empty e of Ridgway's horseshoe. Attached to parts of the 3rd Armored Division, 509th Parachute Infantry Battalion and the 1/517th fought furious and cos melees to stymie encirclement. A third enemy force, the 2nd SS Panzer D sion, was trying to slip past Ridgway's southern flank. After brushing the 508 the "Das Reich" veered into the territory of the 325th GIR, pushing it ba Gavin and the 2/504th went to assist in straightening the line. On the morn of the 23rd, glidermen met the stormtroopers at the crossroads of Barac de Fraiture in a savage encounter.

Little deterred in their drive for Manhay, the next day the panzers' ap rent strength made Ridgway unhappily comply with Monty's handwring advice to make a tidier defensive line. The beat-up horseshoe was pulled ti to go from Trois Ponts southwest to Manhay. The 82nd's part of the pull-ba went smoothly, but 7th Armored units were in disarray after the St. Vith deal — the Germans' pounding caused elements to fall apart and run for Ironically, the same Christmas Eve, Peiper gave up hope and ordered remaining troops to destroy their vehicles and walk out.

When the tankers were sent back to recapture Manhay, they had pull themselves together. But, though they got points on the scrappy SS-men the Christmas Day rematch, they could not beat them. Ridgway saw that A borne Infantry was needed, and called in the 3/517th to finish the job.

By 26 December, the Nazis' gamble had failed. They would never get Antwerp or even Liege. Even to hold on to their hard-won salient, Bastog would be essential, and it was denied them.

THE BATTERED BASTARDS OF BASTOGNE

The famous drama of Bastogne had begun on 18 December. As the 101st rived, loose-ends elements of the 9th and 10th Armored Divisions met the slaught at outlying hamlets. On the morn, the 501st RCT set out in drizzle d fog to develop the situation. Contact came close in at Neffe, where some nkers were cut off. The Geronimo battalions moved forward aggressively, tting up the strongest fight the foe had yet encountered. The advance guard the 26th Volksgrenadier Division passed the word — and their main forces ose to bypass Bastogne for the moment. The Airborne too was impressed the bloody tussle and went on the defensive where it stood.

In the north, the 1/506 fought a similar fight, against lead elements of the d Panzer Division above Noville. But there were just too many panzers. e eerie, frozen night of 19-20 December found the 1/506 and the 3/506 Foy, beating off probes and praying for dawn. At daylight, Nazi artillery t their measure and the attack came. Fog helped bazookamen keep the nzers at bay, before Noville was cut off, and again when the time for withawal came. On the west, the 2/327th played out a like episode at Marvie. ough no triumphs, these skirmishes helped upset the enemy timetable.

This C-47 was one of eight craft with volunteer crews from the 94th Troop Carrier Squadron, 439th TC Group on the resupply flight to Bastogne on the morning of 27 December. Itself loaded with paradrop bundles and towing a glider loaded with artillery ammo, "Ain't Misbehavin' " was hit and set on fire. But pilot Lt. Ernest Turner held steady until his loads were free, then had his crew bail out. Alone, he rode the plane all the way in and came to rest in the 463rd PFAB sector. For his heroism he received the Distinguished Flying Cross.

ter an all-night affray, men of the 101st (possibly 1/502nd) set out to rejoin eir outfit in the morning dawn. They carry rations and blankets from the comand post's supply dump, thanks to recent deliveries via air express. (U.S. Army)

The siege of Bastogne was marked by shortages of fuel, ammunition (especially for the artillery fatefully stranded inside the "doughnut"), and wherewithal to care for the growing numbers of wounded. Armored vehicles had to move about sparingly. With many more vehicles carrying organic loads of shells, the non-Airborne gunners had fair amounts of fodder, but not so the pack 75's and 105's. The 101st's 326th Airborne Medical Company had been taken over by Nazi infiltrators in mainly civilian clothing, and swallowed whole — 142 medics taken prisoner, its equipment destroyed. Medical care throughout the siege was a makeshift operation.

Fortune at last favored the 101st. The "Siberian Express," a high pressure weather front out of Russia, brought clear skies and hard-frozen ground. Air support became possible, and the Troop Carriers laid on 400 resupply sorties, while 1,000 were flown by fighters and bombers. The freeze also helped speed Patton's relief forces.

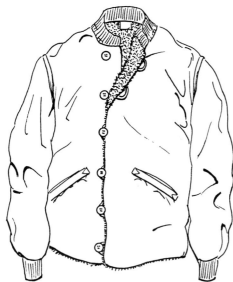

The pile liner was rushed into service when it became obvious troops did not care to wear the intended "Ike" (wool field jacket) under the M1943 field jacket. It did not button into the field jacket and was sometimes worn as an outer garment.

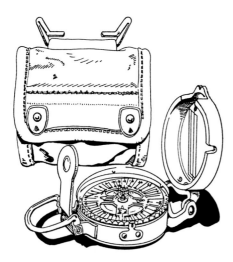

The lensatic compass was usually issued only to officers and NCO leaders. The carrying pouch illustrated was not a Quartermaster-issue accoutrement. Like the compass it was issued with, it was a Corps of Engineers item, and was designed to be secure and water repellent. In this it succeeded too well: getting the compass in and out was so awkward that most users threw the official pouch away and used the simpler first aid packet carrier or a pocket. As it was an expensive, accountable item that was easily lost (aside from its practical uses in urgent situations), the custom soon began of tying it to one's person with a bootlace "idiot rope."

The final chapter of the Bastogne epic was written when the Screaming Eagles plunged through the crust of the German resistance and headed north to Houfalize. The enemy tenaciously tried to hold onto his escape routes and the fighting was not easy. Here a crew of the 463rd PFAB serves their piece during the break-out. (U.S. Army)

The battle for Bastogne peaked on Christmas Eve and the next two days as it did in Ridgway's bailiwick. The big attack came early on Christmas. The Germans knew the weakest sector: where the 502nd PIR and 327th lines joined on the northwest. With thick fog negating air support, their gains were substantial. But again fortune smiled on the Screaming Eagles. On the 26th, 289 resupply sorties made it. The ammo delivered was put to use the next day devastating the Wehrmacht's last, desperate effort to crush the enclave of Bastogne. Late in the day, a task unit of the 4th Armored Division (under future Army Chief of Staff Creighton Abrams) bulled through the infestation of Huns. At Assenoi southwest of the bastion they were greeted by the 326th Airborne Engineers.

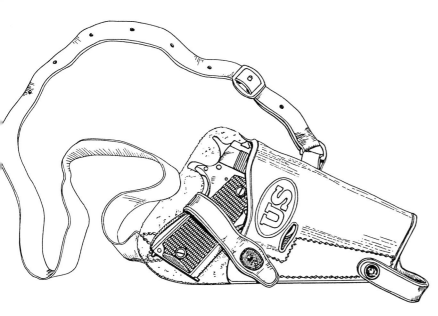

...e .45 automatic pistol was designed by John Browning and first mass-produced ...the commercial M1905 by Colt. An improved version was adopted by the U.S. ...litary in 1911 and won fame in WWI. Modifications adopted in 1926 resulted ...the M1911A1, first produced in quantity in 1937. The M-3 shoulder holster (here) ...as configured to hang below the wearer's armpit and had a limited adjustment ...nge; late in the war, it was supplanted by the M-7, which laid across the left ...east and had longer adjustable straps that even allowed wearing it around the ...aist.

Though the encirclement was broken, and the link-up was quickly solidi-...d, the battle for Bastogne was not over. Further attacks ordered by the ...uhrer materialized as patrols and company-sized probes of the perimeter, ...d night bombing attacks. But the respite — during which supplies and re-...forcements came up the relief corridor and dead, wounded refugees and ...isoners went out — ended on New Year's Eve. The heaviest air raids yet ...sisted renewed thrusts. In coordinated assaults on 3 January, most of the ...01st's line (now shrunken, with armored units responsible for the southern ...ird of the doughnut) felt the wrath of the desperate enemy. This too failed.

As this event unfolded, the First and Third Armies began their counter-...fensive to squeeze The Bulge flat between them. As a participant in what ...as to prove some of the fiercest fighting of the campaign, the 17th Airborne ...vision got its baptism of fire. Two "leg" divisions were demoralized and ...auled in a meeting engagement with German units intent on assailing Bas-...gne from the west. The Golden Talon was haphazardly propelled into the ...each, into a bitter, surrealistic battle.

Paratroopers of Edson Raff's 507th "Spider" PIR greet cavalrymen of VII Corps upon link-up of the First and Third Armies at LaRoche, Belgium, on 14 January 1945. Larry Becker of the S-2 shop wears a British Denison jump smock, another the M1942 jump jacket. (U.S. Army)

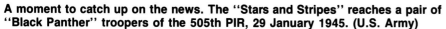

A moment to catch up on the news. The "Stars and Stripes" reaches a pair of "Black Panther" troopers of the 505th PIR, 29 January 1945. (U.S. Army)

Arctic Overshoes and wool overcoats proved precious to Airborne troops in the Ardennes. As the frontline troops hit the road north, supply crews left the rest camps for depots around Paris to find winter gear and get it expeditiously forward. When the trucks caught up with the Airborne units, they slowed but did not halt — coats, shoes and blankets were broken out of bales and tossed off the tailgates to foot-slogging soldiers — sorting out sizes was thereafter the problem of the individual customer.

66

...e Reconnaissance Platoon of the 101st Airborne Division, spring 1945. Roughly ...lf its personnel were parachute-qualified, but by this time it did not matter and ...ams and Sections were intermingled. (Earl R. Price)

As a howling storm hit, the 17th stoically floundered into the whiteness ...the woods. As their Screaming Eagle brethren were beating off the last ...tack on their perimeter, the 194th GIR and 513th PIR led the way in ruining ...e would-be western pincer. The 513th PIR — noted as an Expert Infantry ...it because it had qualified most of its men for that then-new badge in En-...and — moved on Flamierge aggressively.

Through awful weather and heavy barrages, using bayonets and grenades ... root the foe out of fighting positions concealed under snowdrifts, and "tank ...ller" bazooka teams to deal with numerous tanks, Coutts' "Black Cats" ...shed on. The 466th PFAB knocked out tanks that stopped atop one battery's ...servation post. In the whiteout, they fired blind, directed by the battery com-...ander conducting business *under* the targets. When ammunition ran short, ...e paratroopers took up captured ordinance.

The glidermen — not able to find any of the adjoining leg units to tie in ...ith — were enfiladed with murderous fire. A hallmark of the 17th's Belgian ...areer was the lavish use and unusual lethality of artillery and mortars un-...ashed by the enemy. The Wehrmacht was using up its ammo stocks, to ...uy time for withdrawal and to avoid hauling it out. Worse yet, overwhelmingly ...eir rounds were air bursts, detonated by the treetops of the forested terrain.

...rior to MARKET-GARDEN, the 82nd and 101st conjured up provisional Recon-...aissance Platoons, which were formalized by T/OE in December 1944. These ...ad 17 jeeps and 12 motorcycles, and over 60 personnel organized as two Sec-...ons of two squads each. The 82nd's jeeps were "heavied-up" with field-...xpedient armor and .50 caliber guns. The platoon HQ operated one maintenance ...ep and two radio-jeeps with mid-range SCR-694's mounted over the left rear ...heel. These, and their operators who sat sideways on the opposite wheel well, ...ere shielded by additional panels of steel plate. The 101st eschewed the armor-...ate and heavy machine gun and normally substituted .30 caliber guns, often ...ounted on a cut-down pintle in the front passenger seat area. The 82nd rec-...gnized the disadvantages of the .50 — its considerable muzzle blast could tem-...orarily deafen and blind both driver and gunner — but revered its "big voice" ...r scaring the daylights out of German sentries unlucky enough to challenge ...eir patrols.

Officers' Call in the 325th Glider Infantry, probably late January 1945. Left to right: Cpt. William H. Hall, S-1; Lt. Col. Charles W. Major, Commanding Officer of 2nd Battalion; Lt. Col. Teddy H. Sanford, CO 1st Battalion; Col. Charles Billingslea, Regimental CO; unidentified; Maj. Richard M. Gibson, Executive Officer, 2nd Battalion; and (wearing Silver Star Medal) Cpt. Junior Woodruff, CO of Company F. The medal was awarded for actions at Barque de Fraiture versus the 2nd SS Panzer Division.

For its gallant stand at Bastogne the entire 101st Airborne Division received t Presidential Unit Citation. Here, on the occasion of its presentation on 15 Mar 1945, Gen. Eisenhower troops the line of selected soldiers who shared his hor states (Kansas and Texas) — their hometowns displayed on stencilled tapes we on their pocket flaps. The assortment of helmet marks is noteworthy. (U.S. Arn

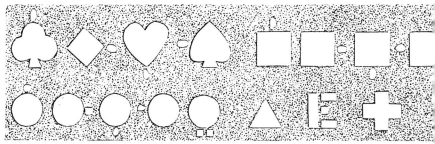

101st markings: HHC, 327th GIR; 1/501st PIR; 2/502nd PIR; 3/506th PIR; Div HI 501st Abn Sig; 426th Abn QM; 801st Abn Ord; HHB, DivArty; 321st GFAB; 37 PFAB; 907th GFAB, 463rd PFAB; 81st Abn AAA; 326th Eng; and 326th Abn M

On 7 January, the 17th renewed the battle of "Deadman's Ridge." The 193rd and 194th took the forested flanks, replete with more infernal bombardment and heavy losses. Now savvy to the local rules, 3/513th waded across a trough of open fields, through a mile of knee-deep snow, into the teeth of the German defense. With a tardy supporting barrage crashing down just ahead, they took the town in pitched hand-to-hand combat. The rest of the Black Cats and 3/507th tried to move up to reinforce, but contact was tenuous at best.

The next morning, the Germans counterattacked through the frozen hell with everything they had — tanks, flakguns, self-propelled guns, flamethrowers, and nebelwerfers included. Cut off, the battalion gave as good as it got through the day and night. Ultimately, it was ordered to exfiltrate. Casualties ran to half the unit lost.

VARSITY: FORGOTTEN FINALE

Once The Bulge was flattened, the Allies faced the need to cross the Rhine. ven with the lucky toehold at Remagen, this natural barrier had to be passed nd havoc wreaked in the heart of the Reich if victory were to be assured.

Brereton, the visionary who had plotted for the vertical envelopment of ortress Metz a war before, was now a man of power. The staffs of his First irborne Army were hungry for targets and hatched a scheme, for example, o overwhelm the Ruhr industrial region with a strategic encirclement from e sky. Called Operation ARENA, this would have inserted four American nd two British Airborne Divisions, their controlling Corps echelons, and four irlifted infantry divisions. Though no doubt dazzled by all this, Ike no doubt ad the Promise vs. Delivery vicissitudes of MARKET-GARDEN in mind when e directed a more modest revision. As an adjunct to an amphibious event - Operation PLUNDER — the XVIII Airborne Corps would conduct an attack, the domain of Eisenhower's chum Field Marshal Montgomery.

At Wesel, the U.S. 17th Airborne Division and the British 6th Airborne Di- sion were to land between the Diersfordt forest and the next-deeper Issel iver, seize high ground and bridges, and otherwise confound the Nazi de- nse and abet the advance of the waterborne forces. Lessons learned from oth Holland and Normandy guided the planners. Both divisions would be rought in whole, except for truckborne service elements which would be await- g link-up on the friendly shore. The airhead would be compact, not strung ut in pieces, but reaching beyond the horizon. On tap would be artillery assed Russian-style along the river, and air force teams accompanying the irborne would be in constant touch with fighters and aerial resupply units aiting in "cab ranks." Hoping that the Germans would be counting on the irborne to lead the attack, hence pinpoint the main effort, the authorities cheduled the amphibious assault first, before dawn; to minimize confusion,

n a pre-VARSITY rehearsal, Lt. William Stary of H/513 gives final instructions. t left, a probable light machine gun is carried in a locally-made bag, a can of mmo strapped to it.

he Airborne Kitbag was invented by the British as a means of jumping heavy ear with troops. It was first taken up by the American Airborne on "reverse end-Lease" in North Africa. It was positioned either across the chest (for deli- ate contents such as radios) or resting atop the right foot and strapped to the ght leg. Because its awkwardness chanced a hang-up in the door, usually no ore than the first two men in a stick could use the kitbag. Once the user's chute ad opened and stabilized, the bag could be released from the leg by pulling e pin on the canvas and leather rig and lowered on its 20-foot line. In this fash- on, the weight was separated from the parachutist's body; the length of the line as computed to allow the bag to be on the bounce at the instant the jumper it the ground, but this syncopated motion was sometimes subject to mishap.

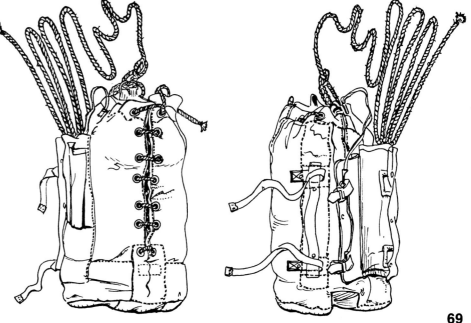

Fierce braves of the Black Cat tribe ready themselves for the Wesel warpath. (Gene Harvey)

Glidermen of the 17th finalize their manifests, 23/24 March. In accordance w... Division S.O.P., they wear no patches or rank insignia on their outer garmen... The man at right mixes the tan M1942 jump trousers with the new green fi... jacket.

While marking time in marshalling areas, members of Company H, 507th PIR gave each other Mohawk haircuts and began using black camouflage paint to make crude Black Widow spiders (the regimental totem) on their faces. On the suggestion of the commander, the unit artist, Bob Baldwin, took up a theatrical makeup kit to decorate ten or more men in full-color detail. Once on the ground at Wesel, most of the fearsome paint jobs could no longer be recognized as spiders; due to smearing and washing away in sweat, nondescript tiger-stripes of black and orange were all that remained. However, platoon sergeant Vic Nielsen, wounded and medevacked to England by air, found that his makeup lasted just fine — it was the object of much jesting amongst nurses and flight crews, and not cleaned off until surgery. (Illustration by Robert M. Baldwin)

Airborne would not arrive on the scene until six hours after dawn. With
big airlift soaking up troop carrier inventories, USAAF bombers were
arged with resupply. It is noteworthy that the 13th Airborne Division was
have a part, but its projected landing on the far side of the Issel was thought
bridge too far'' and the requisite airplanes better used elsewise.

When alerted for VARSITY, the 17th Airborne Division was still enmeshed
the epilogue of Bulge combat in Luxembourg. Led by Maj. Gen. William
ey (who commanded the pioneer 501st Parachute Battalion in 1940), the
olden Talon'' withdrew to camps at Chalons, near Paris, to prepare. The
itish 6th was back home after its Bulge venture. Both busied themselves
relearning the parachute and glider trades. The 17th absorbed 4,000 new
ops, its problems redoubled by sweeping reorganization just going into
ect.

A good view of equipment, as visiting Generals hitch a ride with the 466th PFAB
for a combat jump. Brig. Gen. Josiah Dalbey, former supremo of the Stateside
Airborne Command and chief of staff of the First Airborne Army, and Brig. Gen.
Ridgeley Gaither, on temporary duty from his position as commander of Ft. Benning Parachute School, affect freshly-appended cargo pockets. Dalbey's boots
are the uncommon pre-war staff officers' field boots. Gaither makes do with the
M1943 field jacket liner as an outer garment — and a leather pistol magazine
pouch intended for dress wear. Lt. James Nammack, kneeling at right, wears
the M1942 jump suit with a gauze arm flag and has taped two magazines to the
forearm of his Thompson. (U.S. Army)

nd Grenades: the Mark II ''pineapple'' fragmentation model, the Mark I illum-
ating grenade (a Navy standard, usually associated with amphibious landings),
Mark IIIA1 concussion type, and the M-18 smoke signal.

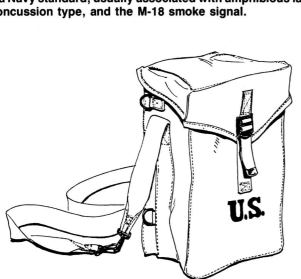

The General Purpose Ammunition Bag was originally developed to carry belted
machine gun ammo and grenades, but found wider usage. Always looking for
ways to carry more than the musette bag and jump suit pockets could hold, paratroopers tended to stuff it with the heaviest loads possible — if and when these
broke away during jumps, they were lethal projectiles.

Paratroopers of the 513th PIR climb into the whale-like C-46 by ladder. An alternative means of entry was a wooden ramp. (U.S. Army)

Rigging the C-46 for dropping parapacks proved a problem. With a cruising spe that equalled the flat-out maximum of the C-47 (230 mph) and different slipstre patterns, the usual arrangements got the bundles ripped away or jammed the racks. The solution was a field expedient to fabricate nose-shields from dr tanks meant for fighters. (U.S. Army)

This, effective 1 March 1945, reversed the official 2:1 ratio of glider to parachute elements in all U.S. Airborne Divisions. At the regimental level, this saw the assignment to the 17th of the veteran 507th PIR, joining the 513th PIR. To fit the new pattern, just one of the two extant Glider Infantry Regiments would continue, and it would have three line battalions plus support elements akin to those of "leg" units. The 194th GIR designation lived on, while the 193rd nameplate was retired. The latter, with the attached 550th Glider Infantry Battalion (a long way from its birthplace in Panama) had been badly chopped up in January and were sadly undermanned. The personnel and equipment of both were stirred into the Division.

More subtly, manning in infantry units was increased and the artillery fectively doubled. In addition to direct support field artillery battalions for ea infantry regiment, a fourth was devoted to general support. All had three ing batteries in place of the former two. For dealing with the panzers, antita weapons were augmented, with bazookas climbing from 186 to 567 (theor cally, as more than 300 had in reality been hauled around since Norman The old establishment of 8,520 troops (not counting the accustomed atta ments) was supplanted by a complement of 12,979. The old division had depend on 302 jeeps and just 104 trucks; the new had 750 jeeps and 2 trucks, including some deuce-and-a-half. Where the 1943 organization co be packed into 181 C-47's and 707 CG-4A's, the 1945 type needed 445 a 997, respectively.

With sunrise on Saturday, 24 March 1945, 667 USAAF transports r around Paris. Loaded with jumpers and towing 906 Wacos (of which ab 600 were in double-tow), this stream rendezvoused with the British-ori lift over Belgium. This was the largest combat airlift ever. An aweso advertisement for airpower in the clear, cold skies, it took nearly two an

the ground at Wesel, what appears to be a Britisher (possibly a glider pilot :onded from the RAF) in Yank clothing helps keep an eye on the developing uation. His helmet is British, with leather earflaps and radio earphones, while weapon is a Mark V STEN gun. His American partner has an M-3 knife or M-4 fe-bayonet in the very lately adopted M-8A1 scabbard.

The simultaneous two-door exit feature of the Curtiss abetted rapid egress. Given the combination of vulnerable fuel system and heavy German flak to "torch" the ship, VARSITY jumpers soon came to appreciate this. Here two kitbags are in use. The C-46 transported a maximum of 40 jumpers versus the C-47's top load of just 21. (U.S. Army)

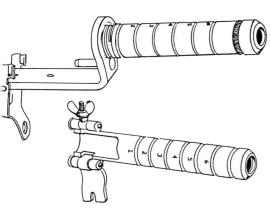

The M-7 (upper) and M-8 (lower) grenade launchers were for the M-1 Garand rifle and M-1 carbine, respectively. With the grenade pushed all the way down, ranges of 365 and 285 yards were possible.

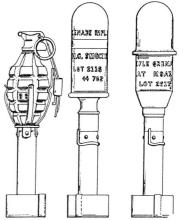

Rifle Grenades: the M-1 projection adapter with Mark II fragmentation grenade, the M-20 Heavy Cloud smoke type, and the M-9A1 antitank type.

Safely on the ground at Wesel and no doubt eager for a fight, an unidentified group of glider pilots acting as "Very Light Infantry" under the control of the 53rd Troop Carrier Wing. Glider pilots for the 17th include borrowed British RAF powered-plane and American fighter pilots. Four "yellow sweatrags" are visible.

The "yellow rag" identification panel of chartreuse-colored silken cloth was issued to glider pilots and troops of the 17th Airborne Division for Operation VARSITY. In theory, it was to be worn draped over troops' backs to mark them as "friendlies" for close-support aircraft, or tied across their fronts when expecting to link up with compatriots. In reality, such uses only drew fire from the enemy; the panels soon were relegated to service as "sweat rag" neckerchiefs.

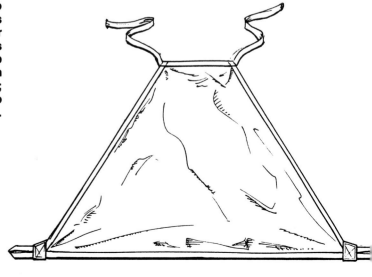

Under the wing of a Horsa glider on the LZ, Capt. Fuss of the 17th Airborne Division G-3 shop models a maroon beret (with rank badge) and Denison smock (with "chicken claw" patch). (Turner Fuss)

VARSITY D+4: Troops of the 194th GIR move on after setting a sniper-ridden
barn ablaze. The light-colored scarves in evidence are not pieces of parachutes,
but rather chartreuse yellow identification panels.

half hours to pass over spectators arrayed on the western bank of the Rhine.
These included Generals Brereton and Ridgway, plus their superiors, Ike and
Churchill. Sightseers Gavin and Omar Bradley orbited high above. The air
show included approximately 900 escort fighters and another 1,200 working
over anything suspicious near the objectives. Beyond sight, thousands of
bombers were inviting what was left of the Luftwaffe to stay away.

Though destined to be the "best" Airborne operation of the war, VAR-
SITY was not without difficulties. When the troop carriers dropped down to
600 feet for the run-in, the billowing smokescreen meant to cloak the river-
crossing obscured marker panels and colored smokepots set out on the near
shore by grounded Pathfinders. Worse, smoke and dust raised by bombardment disguised the drop zones. To further impede accuracy, and contrary
to guarantees, Wesel was still rich in flak. Though Allied strikes and the Germans' perception that the main attack would be to the north had diverted
many of the big guns and tanks and first class infantry), lighter stuff abounded.
Rebuked for ducking fire in earlier missions, determined pilots foreswore evasive action and plunged onward.

The first paratroopers to arrive were the 507th PIR and its associated
464th PFAB. The leading serials had surprise working for them, and the "Spiders" had a fairly good drop. Just the 1st Battalion was far from DZ "W,"
by a mere mile. The regimental commander was Col. Edson Raff, who had

VARSITY D+1, Bruen, Germany: XVIII Airborne Corps boss Matthew B. Ridgway
and British officers chat with Col. Bill Moorman, G-4 of the Corps staff (who wears
an M-3 shoulder holster adjusted to its maximum length to ride on his hip). The
Briton at left wears a "RIFLE BRIGADE" shoulder title and carries a Canadian
Inglis-Browning Hi-Power pistol.

led America's first combat jumps in North Africa back in 1942. "Little Cae-
sar" Raff collected his gang of "Ruffians" and began subduing enemies
in the DZ neighborhood, first falling upon a unit of 150mm guns. His 2nd
Battalion landed under fire, but in good order, then moved out smartly. Against
opposition "averaging moderate," it linked up with British Royal Marine
Commandos advancing from the river that afternoon. The 3/507 was also

75

VARSITY was the combat debut of the 57mm recoilless rifle that was a great improvement over the cranky and inaccurate bazooka. While the 75mm RR was assigned to the antitank companies of the glider infantry regiments, the smaller weapon was organic to parachute infantry — initially issued in addition to the complement of bazookas. (U.S. Army)

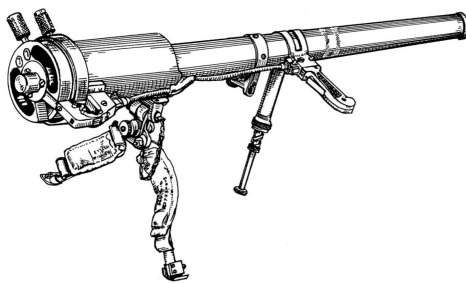

The chief disadvantage of all recoilless rifles such as the M-18 57mm "reckless" is their backblast. Bystanders could not hope to go unscathed inside a triangular area at least 50 feet behind and firing in an enclosed space would at least deafen and daze the crew. The German airborne had used the first RR's notably in the battle for Crete in 1941.

delivered in nice fashion, but its labors proved more difficult. Action center on the Diersfordt castle, which it turned out was the command post of Germans' LXXXVI Corps and 84th Infantry Division. The result of savage clo combat at that strongpoint was 500 prisoners, among them dozens of c cers, and five tanks knocked out. No one was counting the Nazis killed run off. The 464th PFAB was somewhat dispersed and found three of its piec inoperable. But the other nine were quickly put into service, along with a f .50 caliber machine guns. Pummeling the woodlines with these made it pl that DZ "W" was going to stay in *Amerikaner* hands. The "Black Cat" 513 PIR under Col. James Coutts (a Captain in Miley's old 501st Battalion) w next to hit the silk. Unfortunately, what Germans had not popped up to on the first wave of transports made amends to greet the chubby C-46's. 72 Curtiss Commando transports ran into a wall of fire, with terrible effe Nineteen crashed or blew up in the sky. Coutts' own plane was stream flames as it passed over the river, and got worse before the green light ca on. As sure death as the blazing ship was, the fireworks on the way do and the batteries of 88's raking the Z were little better. Coutts' plane exploc as the jumpers looked above to check their canopies.

Not mysteriously, the 513th was misdropped. It was plunked down th miles northeast of where it belonged, on LZ's populated with His Majest air-landing chaps. As fierce fighting prevented an immediate striking out the correct turf, Coutts and Company waded in. It took hours for things quiet down before the 513th could go about its assigned tasks. Their shar of battle with the Britons was paralleled by casual help from errant 507th a 194th troopers and gaggles of marauding glider pilots in softening up its o objectives. As 1/513 secured the LZ, the 2/513 pushed through the thick of the Diersfordt to take a vital ridge in a night assault. After taking a wro road, the 3/513 swung back to wrest the Issel bridges from the Boche bef dusk and made contact with the British.

The artillery of the 513th RCT, the C-47-delivered 466th PFAB, had odd misfortune of landing right on DZ "X," only to discover a conspicu shortage of friendly infantry. Before they could hope to cock any cannon, th had to fight for their lives. All officers of one battery were felled in short ord Rallying, the Redlegs (reinforced by passing packs of glidermen) manag to hold off the foe and assemble their guns. Within 30 minutes, they w paying back the enemy. One player in this drama was a general on a busma holiday from a safe assignment back in the States. Brig. Gen. Josiah Dalb head of the Camp Mackall Airborne Training Command had the dubious ho of leading an agglomeration of American and British glider pilots in a tus with 20 mm *flakwagens!* Once in radio contact with the 513th main for the 466th covered its link-up — firing from behind the enemy, toward the bound infantry being supported.

The glider effort was beset by some of the worst air turbulence possil but the very compact, unintentionally low-altitude delivery of 3,942 gli soldiers (double-towed in 578 CG-4A's) to LZ "S" greatly helped the bi struggle for possession. This area bordered by the forest, the Issel, an canal was infested with Wehrmacht artillery positions and a modicum entrenched or concealed infantry. Taught to unleash everything they had landing gliders, they did so. The hot-and-heavy encouraged soldiers of C

ɔb" Pierce's 194th GIR to charge off the LZ ASAP, with blood in their eyes.
s phenomenon the enemy had not been told about, and the rush was so
t that as a freshly captured Nazi commander was being ushered out one
ɔr of his bunker, his orderly came in another to remind his boss not to for-
his maps!

Unlike the dogfaces, the gunners of the 680th and 681st GFAB's could
hug *terra firma* and wriggle off to bash the *Boche.* They had to stay and
ɔose themselves (mostly on hands and knees) to extract their howitzers
n the tattered and shattered Wacos. Despite the destruction of 40 gliders
the LZ, six 105's and some antitank guns of the 155th Airborne AAA/AT
talion were duelling with the Krauts within the hour — one more thing the
ɔerts from Berlin had not mentioned to the *volksgrenadiers.*

Just before noon, another glider wave headed for DZ "N" with 302 Wa-
;. This increment was comprised of the 139th Airborne Engineer Battalion
;s its jumper companies working with their designated PIR's) and a mis-
any of support units. It expected to find the LZ protected by the 513th
ₗ. But, released too high, it was soon clear that the infantrymen below were
;tile. Heavy fire ripped the fragile gliders ruthlessly. With few protests from
;sengers, pilots took drastic action to get down pronto. The barnstorming
wl was long remembered. From the helter-skelter airhead, squads de-
ıched and returned fire. With Engineers (who had the most tactical skill
those present) as the sparkplugs, this had the fortuitous effect of sand-
hing the Germans between the late arrivals and the prowling "Black Cats"
he 513th. The foe was vanquished.

Aside from the inauguration of new tables of organization, the control in-
ations for the airlift, the entrance of the 17th into the pantheon of Airborne
ry, and the debut of the C-46 in ETO combat, VARSITY boasted other firsts.
ₑ use of the selective-fire M-2 version of the carbine (by at least some glider
ₗlerymen) may have been its introduction to combat anywhere. The 57mm
ₗ 75mm recoilless rifles saw their baptism of fire, the former knocking out
ₑ tanks for the 3/507 at the castle. The larger "reckless" weapon was used
the 155th AAA/AT against various targets, but records give no details. Air
ₑe control teams brought in by glider vectored in fighter strikes (these were
ₑish TENTACLE parties, as the USAAF counterparts were scheduled to
ₑe on follow-up lifts that were scrubbed as unnecessary). For the first

diers of the 513th PIR make themselves small while waiting for the word to
ˈance on Munster, 2 April 1945. Sherman tanks of the Coldstream Guards sup-
ˈting the move are draped with "yellow sweatrags." One trooper has covered
 helmet with camouflaged parachute silk and another wears an M-4 knife-
ˈonet (note the muzzle ring) on his calf. (U.S. Army)

 squad leader divvies up the PX goodies: Company E, 194th GIR, Munster.
ₜ to right: T-5 Wong Chice, Sgt. Tom Canada, Pvt. Clark Tyler, PFC Raymond
ˈelastro, PFC Alfred Ribiccio, SSgt. Earle Ringler, PFC Hershel Harrison, and
 Richard Smolinski. (U.S. Army)

In Munster, troops of the 17th converse with Scots Guards crewmen of a British Churchill V tank (armed with a 95mm howitzer). (Dick Reardon)

time, contributions of U.S. glider pilots as "very light infantry" were worth bragging about. Whereas their British brethren had long been trained to secure and oversee LZ's, defend command posts, and handle prisoners, the orphan American kite-drivers had not had such a directed purpose. In this case, the 53rd Troop Carrier Wing set up a battalion headquarters of sorts to form up and dispatch to needy sectors gaggles of clipped-wing birdmen. Of about 1,770 G.P.'s in VARSITY, 35 died, 85 were wounded, and 55 unaccounted for.

VARSITY involved an unprecedented one-shot airlift of 21,680 Airborne troops, 9,387 of them Americans. Casualties in the 17th were 223 dead in the assault, plus about 136 more during the first day's fighting. (Statistics vary, depending on source, with disagreements probably due to imprec timeframes). The 17th counted 522 wounded and 840 missing (about 6 of whom turned up the next day). The IX Troop Carrier Command coun 41 killed and 153 wounded among its aircrews, plus 163 missing in acti The operation cost 22 C-46's and 12 C-47's, plus 16 Wacos shot out of sky. But the gliders got it worse on the ground, with just 148 of the 880 t landed for re-use. Though the C-46 was a great workhorse, it proved a f trap, as it lacked the self-sealing fuel cells common in other ETO aircr Once its wing tanks were holed, fuel flowed into the lower fuselage, wh subsequent hits could set it aflame as it sloshed around under the passen compartment. The resupply sorties by B-24 Liberators got mixed reviews with 15 of 240 participants downed and many others damaged. British los were much the same. In the 6th Airborne Division, 347 perished and 731 w wounded. The RAF transport squadrons lost just seven Dakotas, all of th glider tugs. Of the USAAF aircraft dropping paras, 17 did not return. Of ab 400 gliders that made it to the LZ's (35 aborted), just 88 were not hea damaged.

In the aftermath, detractors questioned whether VARSITY was justi at all, suggesting the amphibious spectacle alone could have done the nicely. The Germans, according to 20/20 hindsight, were whipped anyw so the big drop was "just a last hurrah" for those (such as Brereton) seek to aggrandize their Airborne concept. Though not because of the gainsay VARSITY never got the kind of attention heaped on smaller and less peri operations; it was lost in the glare of publicity for Patton's armored jugg nauts engaged down south. But, what if the whole of PLUNDER had met position as strong as that which chewed up the 51st Highland Division wl it slogged ashore north of Wesel? If the Rhine crossing had floundered, Russians might have been met at that river rather than the Elbe.

On the night of the 24th, two German counterattacks hit the lines of 194th GIR. Both were defeated, in part through the contributions of gli pilot detachments. Mopping up was the mission of the morrow, while the uation was still in doubt to the north. Once Monty was satisfied that thi had stabilized there, XVIII Airborne Corps (Lt. Gen. Ridgway's staff broached the Rhine on D-Day) energized the pursuit. Not waiting for truc paratroopers of the 513th PIR joined with the British 6th Guards Armou Brigade for a piggyback tank ride towards Munster. Again the *Wehrma* just could not react fast enough to really matter.

On the 27th, the 194th led the way into the town of Lembeck. Ther encountered stiff resistance, first in the streets, then in the municipal Liberating anything with wheels — and a few horses — for mobility, "Golden Talon" pressed on. At the defiles of Haltern and Dulmen, the 2nd Armored Division took over and the 17th turned back to contend the cities of Essen and Duisburg. At this stage the 194th was detached service with "Task Force Twaddle," grouped around the 95th Infantry Divis

As the flood of POW's swelled, the Airborne assumed the job of guarc and escorting them. On 10 April, the 507th captured munitions mogul H Krupp, then the 194th bagged diplomatic star Franz von Papen. Later, F Marshal Model, the personification of the Teutonic warlord ethic and mas mind of The Bulge, refused to capitulate. After setting his troops free to f or quit as they wished, he committed suicide.

ONWARD INTO THE REICH

In the aftermath of The Bulge, the Airborne slogged on as ordinary, non-escript dogfaces in the campaign to eliminate the German salient and get n with the penetration of the Reich. Under Ridgway's corps, the 82nd and tached 1/551st PIR rolled eastward, confronted the Siegfried Line on the st day of January, and cracked it two days later. Then they were pulled back, d returned to the camps around Rheims on 17 February. The 101st broke ut of Bastogne in mid-January, then on the 18th signed over possession f "their town." Two days later, the division was sent southward to Alsace, hold a piece of the Seventh Army's front until redeployment on 26 Feb-uary. The 17th, after garrisoning Bastogne, turned its attentions to Luxem-ourg and the Siegfried, before heading for Rheims on 10 February.

In the camps, the Airborne units did not simply regroup, retrain, and ab-orb replacements. This lull was marked by big changes in organization. The reation of the First Airborne Army half a year before had put impetus behind hronic gripes that the Airborne Divisions were too small and lightly equipped. When the Ardennes emergency hit, Brig. Gen. Maxwell Taylor was in Wash-ngton to iron out plans for the new model units. One result was the disband-nent of the assorted non-divisional units that had so distinguished themselves, n order to free their surviving manpower for reassignment.

Engineers of the 13th Airborne Division stand to for a Stateside display of the multifarious tools of their trade, including flamethrowers, machine gun, bazooka, mine detector, cratering charges and other demolition gear.

Demolition gear commonly used by the Airborne in combat. The bags are the Demolition Equipment Canvas Carrying Bag and the flimsier Demolition Haver-sack. The Bag held accessories, explosives, or a combination, while the Haver-sack was meant for explosives only — and was often consumed in "satchel charge" events. In either case, to avoid inadvertent catastrophe, blasting caps, fuses and firing devices were carried separately, in field-expedient tobacco and shoe-polish cans stuffed in pockets or ammo pouches. Through 1943, the Air-borne relied on TNT blocks (half and full pound), burning safety fuse and M-1 fuse lighters shown at left. Use of electrical firing materiel — wire (atop the coil of safety fuse), galvanometer, 10-cap blasting machine, special (military) and commercial (here, DuPont) electrical blasting caps — marked a "deliberate" op-eration, usually performed by Engineers rather than "hasty" infantrymen. Plas-tic explosives — in the types of blocks arrayed at the right — were a quantum leap in power and convenience, at first considered Classified Material and avail-able only in small quantities prior to Normandy. By then the following were com-mon (left to right at lower right): M-1 15-second delay fuses, M-2 pull-friction and M-1A1 pressure firing devices for boobytraps, and various makes of M-2 weath-erproof fuse lighters. The reel of "detcord" (commercially "Primacord") at cen-ter and the three detcord clips at far right were needed for large-scale use of "plastique." The Engineer jack-knife, M-2 Cap Crimper pliers and roll of friction tape were de rigueur tools for all demo men.

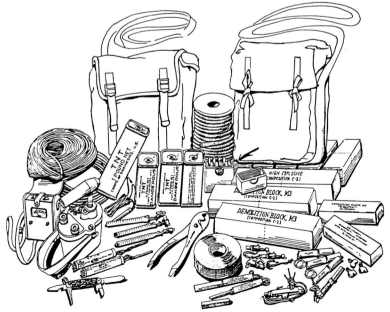

Ready for Operation EFFECTIVE, 13th Airborne Division, April 1945. Desperados of the veteran 517th PIR looking restive at Lille airfield: Pvt. Kimbrough, Cpl. Christensen, PFC Heitten, PFC Schmidt, Cpl. Hammernik; rear: Sgt. O'Malley, PFC Gibson, PFC Pace, PFC Goodbrake and T-4 Childs.

The reorganization (effective 1 March 1945), began with reversal of the two-to-one ratio of glider units to parachute units. The parachute infantry outfits were "heavied up," while the sole-surviving GIR added a 3rd Battalion, a service company and an antitank company. Next, a fourth field artillery battalion was added to provide a general-support capability for the first time, and the engineer and antitank/AAA battalions grew new sub-units. More subtle changes accommodated equipment — vehicles, more bazookas and .50 caliber machine guns, new recoilless rifles, and more. The overall strength of an Airborne Division rose from 8,556 to 12,979.

The 13th Airborne Division, The Golden Unicorn, was activated at Ft. Bragg on 13 August 1943. Its major subordinates were then the 513th PIR, 189th and 190th GIR's, but none of the three regiments stayed long. On 10 March 1944, the 513th "Black Cat" paratroopers transferred out to the 17th Airborne Division (taking the place of the 517th, recently made independent and sent to the Mediterranean Theater) and were supplanted by the 515th "Wolves" (a separate unit under Airborne Command since 31 May 1943). On 4 and 8 December, the more senior 88th and 326th GIR's — non-divisional units until then — pushed the 189th and 190th into disbandment.

Like the older Airborne Divisions, the 13th worked hard, absorbing men and equipment and pushing through the usual training cycle to make ready for overseas service and combat. But it was decimated time after time to pro-

The Devil in Baggy Pants, raising hell across the Rhine. The 504th's PFC Walter Hughes hits Hitsdorf, 6 April. His garb is styled for comfort and speed: old reliable M1942 jump trousers, sweater, a Thompson SMG magazine bag for M-1 clips, a pistol belt in lieu of a rifle cartridge belt, M1918 trench knife, a .45 stuck in a pocket, and British gauntlets. (Walter Hughes)

e M1941 field jacket evolved in 1939-1940 because Maj. Gen. Parsons, the
mmander of III Corps, disliked use of the wool service coat for rough wear.
his behest, the "Parsons jacket" was modelled on existing civilian windbreak-
s. Though an improvement over the brass-buttoned wool coat, it was not a
eat success — troops preferred the "tanker" jacket, longer mackinac, or jump
cket. This example bears the shoulder patch of the 13th Airborne Division and
e unofficial emblem of the 513th PIR. The M1943 field jacket was a product
the ingenuity of the Quartermaster research and development apparatus. The
fspring of a tan ensemble tested in North Africa that was suggested by the
itish bush jacket and the paratroops' jump jacket, it (and other items of the
43 green ensemble) was first issued inside the Anzio beachhead. There, large-
ale tests were conducted by elements of the 3rd Infantry Division — and, un-
ficially, by "Braves" of the 1st Special Service Force who "liberated" theirs
om supply dumps. Stateside authorities intended the new family of clothing
d accoutrements to be in wide use in time for the Normandy campaign, but
e Quartermaster General of the ETO refused to issue it. He insisted old-model
ol clothing, overcoats and leggings were ideal — based on his personal ex-
riences in the trenches of 1918. The new material piled up in the United King-
m until the undeniable need to re-equip the 82nd and 101st after Normandy
d to those units introducing the M1943 types to the ETO.

Topped off with a maroon beret, a member of the Military Police Platoon, 82nd
Airborne Division guards headquarters, spring 1945. (Charles Snyder)

Protocol sentinels at the Grabow townhall, temporary command post of 2/505. George Clarke and Mickey Wargo (coincidentally both veterans of Pathfinder missions) dug out their Class A's on short notice to impress the Soviets. (82nd Airborne Division Museum)

V-E Day, May 1945: Sgt. Adolf Byers of the 17th Airborne Division G-2 sectie displays the Word, clothed in an M1942 jump jacket. (Dick Lacefield)

Maj. Gen. Jim Gavin bestowing a Bronze Star on an already well-decorated Soviet master sergeant of engineers. (82nd Airborne Division Museum)

vide replacements to other units. By the time it deployed to Europe in Jauary 1945, its alumni were numerous everywhere in the Airborne.

In France, based around Auxerre, it was the general reserve of the FA and set aside for several Airborne operations. It was initially programm to take part in VARSITY, but the decision to go with a single airlift exclud it. It then was pegged for CHOKER, a drop behind the Siegfried Line ne Saarbrucken. Its advanced command post was deployed and marshalli proceeding when the job was cancelled. Operation EFFECTIVE, schedule for 20 April, was to help the French advance and nab German scientis reported holed up south of Stuttgart. However, the French broke throug first postponed, the assault was scrubbed on 1 May. The 515th PIR w at one point to be the American contingent in Denmark, with arrival planne by parachute, but this too did not occur.

The 13th left Europe for Ft. Bragg from 15 August 1945 on, kept acti for contingencies in Asia — reinforcement of the invasion of Japan or China, if peace did not dawn gently there. When all the 82nd was hom the 13th (by then understrength) was inactivated on 25 February 1946.

th the coming of warm weather, the 82nd began issuing the unaccustomed d mundane fatigues of green herringbone twill fabric. Here the ever-pugnacious nmy Keenan of Company E, 505th PIR dresses up his wardrobe with a liber- d fireman's belt bearing the coat of arms of the province of Baden-Wurtemberg.

Military Policeman of the 82nd, Germany, 1945. This guardian of law and order ars the red-white-and-blue background trimming of the HQ and Special Troops hind his glider wings. His helmet bears a small replica of the shoulder patch ove the white letters "MP" and the white stripe allotted by regulation to di- ional MP units. (82nd Airborne Division Museum)

The XVIII Corps organized on 10 October 1943 descended from the II Ar- ored Corps, which had overseen training in California. "Airborne" was not plied until Lt. Gen. Matthew Ridgway took command at Ogbourne St. eorge, England, on 27 August 1944.

For MARKET, the Blue Dragon managed logistics and technical support. r The Bulge, its forward element deployed from Epernay, France, to Wer- mont, Belgium; while its rear moved from Ogburne St. George to Epernay. r two months, it controlled parts of six Infantry Divisions, three Armored visions, and a mixed bag of Airborne units.

After The Bulge was flattened, the Corps turned east to the Siegfried line. erations around Roer were cut short to prepare for VARSITY.

Corps Forward deployed to Wesel, Munster and the Ruhr. With four In- ntry Divisions, the Corps conquered the industrial heart of the Reich. On April, "Mission Accomplished" rang out.

Eisenhower next sent Ridgway to spur Field Marshal Montgomery's turtle- e "thrust" onto the North German plain. 21st Army Group was dawdling the Elbe, seemingly set on repeating the GARDEN mess.

Because Monty put the Yanks at the back of the line to cross, Ridgway bverted the plan by scrounging up U.S. engineer units and on the night 29 April forcing the Elbe at Bleckede — five days earlier than Monty said. e 82nd was rushed forward for the job without the say-so of the Brits — trucked, picked up assault boats, and hit the water. The hasty attack caught e Germans (and British) off guard.

Peace found the Corps at Hagenow, awaiting occupation duty in Berlin. t Gen. MacArthur, once he understood VARSITY, asked for the XVIII Corps. 21 May the Dragons began redeploying to Camp Campbell, Kentucky. dgway's advance party was over the Pacific when Japan gave up. The XVIII rps (Airborne) was inactivated on 15 October 1945.

the summer of 1945, one-time Berlin denizen Marlene Dietrich returned home a USO tour. This group of 82nd men had known each other when previously signed to the 17th and got together for the show. Contrary to general practice, embers of the 82nd were discouraged from wearing "combat patches" on the ht shoulder to show their former units, so none of these soldiers display the th patch. (Dick Lacefield)

Cpl. John Heinrich in his going-home duds, M[...] 1945. Though assigned to the gliderborne 681st F[...] he wears the jump wings he earned at Camp F[...] rest in preference to the glider wings with assa[...] landing star his service in VARSITY entitled him [...] He was a "high-pointer" — to prioritize the timi[...] of the release of hundreds of thousands of draftee[...] a system of points based on length of service, ag[...] and married/parent status was devised and put in[...] effect after V-E Day. With the coming of V-J Da[...] virtually any combat veteran who did not enlist [...] the Regulars was marked for return home, w[...] Christmas the "drop-dead date." (John H. Heinric[...]

Veteran of the 325th GIR in Berlin. Although [...] wears the blue-white "oval" behind his wings, [...] does not yet wear the Dutch lanyard (awarded 8 O[...] tober) or Belgian fourragere (22 October). T[...] French forragere was not promulgated until 6 Ap[...] 1946. (William Knarr)

The First Allied Airborne Army sprang from the post mortems of Normandy. Eisenhower wanted not just Airborne Corps, but an even higher headquarters that would be multi-national and permanently group troop carrier units with the Airborne ground forces.

On 2 August 1944, the provisional Combined Airborne Forces was born. After some political wrangling — in which the "majority stockholder" Yanks insisted on an American boss — USAAF Lt. Gen. Lewis Brereton was named commander. Under his hand, the First Allied Airborne Army was formed on 18 August, with headquarters at Sunninghill Park, Ascot.

Its first test was MARKET, the Airborne invasion of Holland. The debacle at Arnhem — or rather the inept planning that led to it — caused Brereton to lose confidence in the British. In the autumn of 1944, a rift developed between U.S. and British members of the FAAA staff, and disagreements during The Bulge widened it.

One manifestation of ill will was an administrative sidestep that on 12 January 1945 separated the Americans of the "Allied" organization and made them HHC, First Airborne Army (U.S. only). Soon thereafter, the h[...] tory of HHC, 1st Airborne Task Force (of Southern France fame) was tak[...] up and perpetuated by the new unit. (The 1ABTF was NOT provisional[...] was a full-fledged TO&E (Table of Organization and Equipment) unit, CO[...] STITUTED 18 July 1944, ACTIVATED three days later, DISBANDED 2 Ja[...] uary 1945, then RECONSTITUTED and CONSOLIDATED with FAA on [...] February).

In the following months, the FAA planned many Airborne operations, sor[...] of which went as far as the planes, gliders and paratroopers marshalled [...] departure fields before being scrubbed. The crowning achievement of F[...] proved to be VARSITY. The multi-national FAAA HQ was dissolved on [...] May 1945, but the American FAA lived on. When XVIII Corps was redirect[...] to the Pacific, the mission of U.S. headquarters for the occupation of Ber[...] passed to FAA. The Berlin District/FAA remained at Maison Lafitte outsi[...] Paris until 1 June, then began its move to Berlin, where it was inactivat[...] 31 December 1945.

in, September 1945: The 2nd Platoon of Company E, 505th Para-
te Infantry, led by Lt. Perkins (right), spruced up like proper Oc-
iers. Note only seven Combat Infantry Badges — and perhaps
EXPERT Infantry Badge on the second from right, front row sol-
— are to be seen, testimony to the transfer out of old hands
transfer in of new guys. (Kenneth Tucker)

Antoine Accristo, 14-year-old "mascot" of the
813th Quartermaster Car Company, First Airborne Army, on the road to Berlin. Tony was a
native of Southern France who had begun killing
Germans two years earlier as a member of the
Maquis. During DRAGOON, he "adopted" a unit
of the 517th PIR and accompanied them in combat into the Alps. Upon the break-up of the 1st
Airborne Task Force, he migrated with his "guardian" to the 813th, a unit that functioned as the
FAA's motor pool. In Berlin, Tony masqueraded
as a midget Sergeant, driving jeeps and trucks
with his G.I. buddies. When an Airborne demonstration was staged for the Soviets, an assault
glider skidded to a stop in front of the reviewing
stand and its load of one gunjeep sped out,
"Sergeant" Accristo at the wheel. An attempt
to stowaway to America at Christmastime 1945
failed, but he later emigrated legally. (Antoine
Accristo)

When his fluency in German became known within HHC, First Airborne
Army, Herb Schumacher's career as a supplyman was curtailed and he
was reassigned to counter-intelligence. In Berlin, he wears properly anomalous and anonymous officer "U.S." brass on the collars of his Ike jacket
and shirt (left), and (right) an undercover disguise as a medical NCO of
troops of the then-demobilizing Wehrmacht.

Nice, Christmastime, 1945: The drill team of the 2/508 waits to enterta[in] the public, decked out in white bootlaces, pistol belts, parachute s[ilk] scarves, and shroud-line aigulettes. Combat Infantry Badges are position[ed] below jump wings, a common practice in the Airborne until regulatio[ns] spelled out proper precedence. (Kenneth Tucker)

Helmet markings: 504th (Holland-Germany); 505th (Mediterranean); 505t[h] (Germany); 508th (Germany); 509th (Italy-Bulge); 551st.

Non-regulation Parachute Infantry guidons in use by the 3rd Battalion [of] the 508th PIR, on the occasion of a visit by President Truman, 4 Ju[ne]. The winged foot helmet markings and the combat patch on the Compa[ny] G guidon-bearer are noteworthy. The latter is that of the First Airbor[ne] Army — in combination with a CIB it suggests the wearer fought in o[ne] of the non-divisional (hence patchless) infantry outfits. (S. William Rya[n])

86

The 82nd Airborne Division was the featured attraction of a "Grand Victory Parade" in New York on 12 January 1946. Before the parade, this Technician 4th Grade attends to the perfect shine of his jumpboots beneath the El tracks. (82nd Airborne Division Museum)

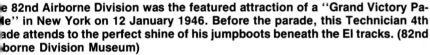

A phalanx of America's Guard of Honor marches through Washington Square in Greenwich Village. All officers in the front rank wear the natty tailor-made version of the Ike jacket in Shade 51 dark olive-green material with contrasting "pink" (beige) trousers, set off by brown gloves and boots.

After more than a year of supernumerary attachment, the 508th PIR was separated from the 82nd Airborne Division to become the guard force of Eisenhower's headquarters city of Frankfurt. In July, sweetheart, figure skater, starlet, and Norwegian patriot Sonja Henie was made an honorary paratrooper and treated to a ride on a demonstration jump from 3000 feet. The chutes are factory-new T-7's with US-style quick release boxes. (U.S. Army)

87

FIRST IN: THE PATHFINDERS

Pathfinders are specialists who form the advance guard of Airborne assaults. They find and occupy landing and drop zones, for the purpose of setting up beacons to guide the main force. The British originated the concept. Their first combat drops showed the need for something new in navigational aids. Their expertise in the infant science of radar led to the invention of the homing devices that were essentials of Pathfinding. In June 1942, they formed the 21st Independent Parachute Company to develop the specialty. In the aftermath of the North African drops, the American 2/509th PIR got wind of the Pathfinding innovations and was interested. By May 1943, when the 21st moved to North Africa, the 509th's provisional Scout Platoon had gotten equipment on "reverse Lend-Lease" to learn the business.

While the 509th was attached to the 82nd Airborne Division, Col. Gavin was especially taken with the Pathfinder idea. But the small quantity of equipment available and lack of work-up time foreclosed the possibility of the "All American" using Pathfinders for the invasion of Sicily — and the foster-child 509th was not invited to the affair.

Subsequently, the blunders of the Troop Carrier flyboys in Operation HUSKY highlighted the need for Pathfinders. After training tests run in August at the Trapani training center, the first three teams were formed in the 82nd. Their success in leading the reinforcement airdrop into the Salerno beachhead was enough to win expanded attention.

By the end of 1943, the new specialty was being studied and improved Stateside and the Airborne units massing in England for the Normandy Invasion were organizing teams of Pathfinders. In the 82nd Airborne Division, each parachute infantry regiment formed three teams, one for each of its battalions, totalling nine altogether. The 101st formed a total of eleven teams, but on the basis of the number of possible Drop Zones, with men from several units intermixed on a team. A team consisted of at least 11 men and often as many as 18 men, with the difference mostly made up of extra security outguards.

Though soldiers accepted for Pathfinder duty were good ones, their status as an elite within an elite was not yet appreciated. For OVERLORD, many were lured by the chance for cross-training in a specialty (on a par with others like heavy weapons, communications, or demolitions) to qualify for promotion — and the safer jobs were already filled! A few were involuntarily detailed by superiors who were out of patience with infractions of discipline — pub-brawling being the chief offense.

Pathfinder duty was temporary, with teams formed only as required for the drops. Indeed, for Normandy the assignment was to end upon the arrival of the main bodies on each Drop Zone, with each member charged with finding his parent company. In practice, however, they would merge with the first group encountered from their own regiment. When it was time to form Pathfinder teams for Holland, old hands who had survived Normandy could not be brought in for the next job against their will or the desires of their parent units.

Pathfinder, 101st Airborne Division, England, January 1944. The waterproof pou hung below this trooper's reserve chute contains the classified EUREKA ra beacon, a device that was sworn at and sworn by among those charged w ensuring the main lifts of Airborne forces arrived on their planned Drop or la ing Zones in good order.

thfinders of the 101st bear up under the gaze of visiting dignitary Winston
urchill and a retinue of correspondents. The Corporal under scrutiny carries
th a hand-axe and machete. In the rear, AN/BUPS beacons and rolled up sig-
l panels can be seen.

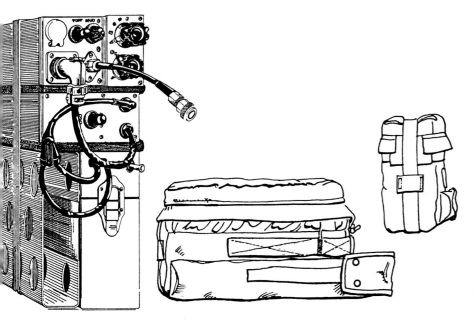

On 23 December, transports holding 20 Pathfinders of the 101st Airborne Division pushed through marginal weather to jump into encircled Bastogne. Coming
to earth between the guns of the 327th GIR and some curious Germans, they
hurried to receive the drop of 1,446 supply bundles scheduled for 90 minutes
later. The need for artillery shells was so acute that some famished guns were
shooting just-unpacked ammo before the drop was over. These Pathfinders had
not been with the Division earlier because they had been detached to the Air
Force Troop Carrier Pathfinder School at Challgrove airdrome in England since
the end of the Holland operation. When called, they saddled up in England. Left
to right: Lt. Schrable D. Williams, John Dewey (nearly covered), Jake McNiece,
Charles H. Partlow, Lochman M. Tillman, Carl Fenstamachter, and atop the brick-
pile John Agnew. (Jake McNiece).

One platoon of 101st Pathfinders, Spring 1945: Front, Richard Wright, Carl Fenstamachter, Jake McNiece, George Blain; Rear: Lt. Schrable Williams, Irving Schumacher, John Agnew, Lochman Tillman, Charles Partlow, James Benson. Not shown are Lt. Gordon Rothwell, John Dewey, Martin Majewsky, Floyd Thomas and William Coad. The team had no authorized vehicles — the motorcycle "mascot" is ex-Wehrmacht, the truck "informally requisitioned" at Bastogne. (Jake McNiece)

Team materiel consisted of two types of radar beacons. "Eureka" sets (AN/PPN-1A) sent coded signals to "Rebecca" receivers installed in planes). BUPS beacons matched up with SCR-717-C sets aloft, but these were less reliable and served as back-ups to the system. Visual signals included "Krypton" pulsating blue lights, flares, smoke grenades, and colored signal panels.

The ascendance of the First Allied Airborne Army led to a greater degree of permanence for the Pathfinders. In October, as the paratroopers regrouped after MARKET-GARDEN, Gen. Brereton directed the IX Troop Carrier Command to combine its 1st Provisional Pathfinder Group with permanent paratroop Pathfinder teams at Challgrove airdrome in England. Each Airborne Division (including the newly arrived 17th) contributed three teams of ten men each.

A Pathfinder of Airborne Command loaded with 110 pounds of BUPS beacon gear. (542nd Parachute Infantry Association via John C. Grady)

When the Germans kicked off their surprise lunge through the Ardennes, [t]he Battle of the Bulge — XVIII Airborne corps units were rushed from rest-[ca]mps in France to counterattack. Their Pathfinder teams were not with them. [Th]is proved a blessing, as when the "Screaming Eagles" were cut off in Bas-[to]gne, their own kind went to their aid.

On 22 December, the 10-man Pathfinder teams of lieutenants Schrable [Wi]lliams and Gordon Rothwell were given a "30 second" briefing on the dire [sit]uation and climbed aboard two planes to fly through rotten weather to the [Ar]dennes. Even the head of the USAAF Pathfinder aircrews, Lt. Col. Joel [C]ouch, could not find Bastogne in the thick blanket of ice fog. Fuel dwind-[lin]g, the search was abandoned for the day.

Before dawn the next day they set out again. The weather was clear over [th]e objective and Williams' team hit the silk first. Coming to earth in the po-[sit]ions of 2nd Battalion, 327th GIR, they popped yellow smoke grenades — [th]e "come on in" signal for having found friendly territory. Rothwell's men [ju]mped on the smoke, while the early arrivals busied themselves with setting [up] a Eureka set on the highest point handy — a brick pile. The resupply DZ [wi]th a T of orange recognition panels laid out by the 101st was considerably [clo]ser to town, and the first serial was right on target. By later afternoon, 241 [tra]nsports dropped 144 tons of supplies. Howitzer ammo was jeeped to gun [pit]s still packed in bundles, some hitting the foe before the last drops.

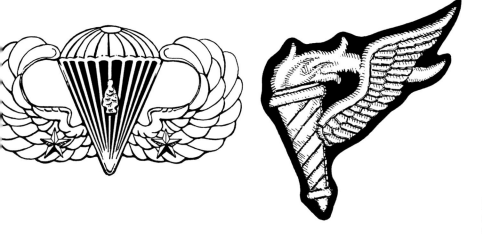

Pathfinder Jim Benson (on detached service from the 506th PIR) brings in a re-supply sortie with an AN/PPN-1A set, at Prum, Germany, 13 February 1945. The 4th Infantry Division had overrun the town, but then found itself cut off from its lines of communication by the enemy on one side and roads and bridges washed away by an early thaw on the other, so required an airdrop of fuel, rations, and engineer supplies. (U.S. Army)

[In] addition to bronze service stars added to the wings to denote combat jumps, [Pat]hfinders used the assault arrowhead device to show Pathfinder missions com-[ple]ted.

[Th]e embroidered cloth Pathfinder badge was approved for wear before Normandy [as] a mark of qualification, but first awarded after OVERLORD for participation [in t]hat operation. By V-E Day, it was given upon completion of the IX TCC Path-[find]er course at Chalgrove.

AIR COMMANDOS: WITH THE CHINDITS IN BURMA

In May 1942, British Empire forces gave up Burma to the Japanese and withdrew to India. In February 1943, a mad-dog Englishman with a fine talent for irregular warfare, Orde C. Wingate, led an experimental "long-range penetration" brigade back into Burma to attack the occupiers. The nascent success of these "Chindits" was relevant to the U.S. Airborne because the jungle fighters were kept going by aerial resupply alone. Inspired by Wingate (and hungry for offensive gains in that somnolent theater) President Roosevelt agreed at the Quebec Conference to underwrite enlarged, strategic "Chindit" ops in 1944 with, among other things, a special task force of American airpower.

The organization that resulted was known successively as "Project 9," the 5318th Special Air Unit (Provisional), and the 1st Air Commando Group (when finally legitimatized by HQ, USAAF). This trailblazing command was formed at Goldsboro Army Air Field, North Carolina, in November 1943. With Washington's (ultimately the White House's) backing, the force scrounged up men and materiel hurried, with its advanced party gaining India the following month.

The Air Commandos were a multi-faceted band of ragged, rugged aviators and machines. Commander Col. Philip G. Cochran had served in North Africa as a P-40 squadron leader and double-duty C-47 flier in association with the equally ragged and rugged 509th Parachute Infantry. Other members were veterans of the "Flying Tigers" American Volunteer Group. Its mainstays were, however, restive noncoms and very junior officers who had earned "second-rate" glider and liaison pilot wings. Such orphans of the Air Corps were eager to join the war but cooling their heels at Stateside bases. Airlift assets at the outset included: 150 Waco CG-4A and 25 TG training-type gliders; 13 C-47 transports; 12 Canadian-made UC-64 Norseman utility planes; a mixture of 103 Vultee L-1 Vigilant (every one available out of a total production run of 324) and L-5 Voyager light craft for liaison and medical evacuation duties; and even six Sikorsky YR-4 helicopters. For tactical air support, there were 33 weary, obsolescent North American P-51A Mustang fighters, considered unsuitable for further training use. In India a dozen B-25H Mitchell bombers packing a panoply of armament in their noses were added, but the hard-won C-47's were yielded to the local troop carrier command.

Like Wingate's 3rd Indian Division (Special Force) and the U.S. counterpart Merrill's Marauders of that 1944 combat season, Cochran's flyboys were meant to operate for just 90 days, then be withdrawn for rebuilding. T

Glider Pilot wings, here with finely detailed feathering. Liaison Pilot wings, like the above authorized 4 September 1942.

Glider pilots at Lalagat, Assam airfield. Some wear shoulder holster strung around their waists. Jump suits were popular not because of their Airborne connections, but simply because they were "bush jackets" with lots of pocket room to carry survival gear. (U Air Force)

92

[m]ajor task of the Air Commandos was the close support of Wingate's air-[bor]ne invasion of Burma; the ground-bound Marauders — working afoot further [no]rth — were not blessed with an equivalent air arm.

The overture for the main landings was a few small-scale glider missions [to] support the advance of cooperating foot-slogging, foliage-whacking columns. [On] 28-29 February, five Wacos in three sorties ("hires" in the local slang, [sh]owing Wingate's view that gliders were nothing more than taxis with wings!) [dro]pped in with raiders and river-crossing boats. Such "hires" resumed after [the] main landings.

For the big event, three LZ's were planned for the 5-6 March job. But at [the] last minute, aerial photos revealed possible enemy interest in LZ PICA-[DIL]LY, and it was not used.

Awaiting the order for landing at Myitkyina, members of the 879th Airborne Aviation Engineer Battalion take shelter under the wing of their Waco. A Chinese-flag "blood chit" adorns the back of a pilot's overalls.

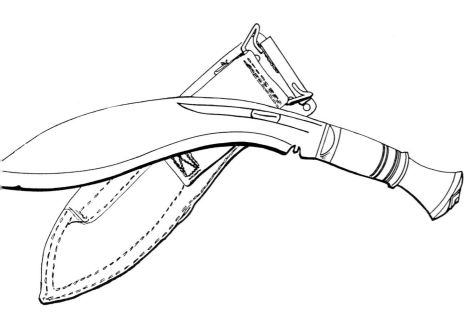

[Th]e kukri was the legendary symbol and personal weapon of the Nepalese Gurkha [so]ldier — suited to lopping off heads, arms, and legs in a single stroke. Mem-[be]rs of the Air Commandos and Merrill's Marauders used them, more as tools [tha]n weapons. This example has a black horn grip and jungle green web scab-[ba]rd with hardware as for machete scabbards.

A few days after the assault on BROADWAY, an Air Commando L-5 is loaded with emergency resupply bundles. The British bush hat and Ghurka kukri (here a scabbard for one is visible on the center figure) were typical of Air Comman-dos. Because Gen. Stilwell insisted "his" CBI patch be worn by every American, the USAAF was moved to the "wrong" sleeve.

93

Orde Wingate and Air Commandos search for inbound transports at CHOWRIN-GHEE LZ. The "biscuit gun" is a signalling device. One airman wears a jump jacket, another jump trousers. At left is a probable anti-aircraft officer equipped with camouflage suit, long pack, British haversack and camo-painted helmet liner.

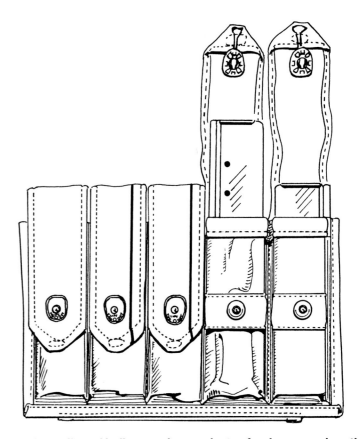

Factories in Australia and India turned out variants of web gear such as this po■ for Thompson magazines. Snap fasteners and other fittings often were impor■ from the U.S.

The first wave of gliders landed more than 150 miles behind Nipponese lines at LZ's BROADWAY and CHOWRINGHEE, carrying Gurkha and British units. American troops were from the 900th Airborne Engineer Aviation Company, essential participants who would use their bantam bulldozers to ready a crude airstrip capable of receiving C-47 squadrons.

Echoing Wingate's disdain for the intricacies of Airborne soldiering, these Chindits (and their mules!) paid scant attention to the instructions of their pilots. The usual load limit for the Waco — 3,750 pounds — had been arbitrarily upped by Wingate's staff, first to 4,000 pounds, then to 4,500. Worse, the troops covertly added even more — "self-provident" overages of food and ammo. Many gliders groaned with 6,000 pound leads, their rather nervous pilots facing double-towing, at night, over wild terrain replete with horrific air currents! More than half the gliders went astray.

94

At BROADWAY, wrecks stopped further landings on the first night. ■ 539 men, 3 mules, and 15 tons of materiel delivered in the blind were enou■ to get things going. Over the next six days, 9,052 men, 175 ponies, and 1,1■ mules, plus 250 tons of cargo were delivered by 581 C-47, 10 UC-64, a■ 74 glider sorties.

Fifty miles south CHOWRINGHEE (named after a Calcutta thoroughfa■ received a dozen Wacos that pushed through mountaintops, downdrafts, a■ a smattering of Jap fire. Their only bulldozer smashed, the 4/9th Ghurka Ri■ got busy with their kukris and machetes to clear 12 acres of undergro■ the hard way. Five more gliders and another dozer came in before da■ Less defensible than BROADWAY, this LZ was abandoned after some ■ transports had unloaded; hours later Japanese planes commenced an att■ that lasted three days.

Here American glider pilots happily join their erstwhile passengers on the legendary "Road to Mandalay."

The British bush hat of Chindit fame was not the same as the wider-brim Aussie slouch. Supplied by contractors in the UK and India, its details varied.

e Clark CA-1 lightweight bulldozer (tractor, crawler type, 20 drawbar horse-wer) was a mainstay of the Airborne Aviation Engineers who carved out landing ips for tactical air forces in several theaters of war. In the 1945 reorganization, was added to the engineer inventory of the Airborne Divisions. Pushing the e and weight limits of the Waco glider, its safe arrival at Broadway was es-ntial to the success of the invasion.

In the bitter and tortuous campaign that ensued, the Air Commandos ac-itted themselves well. They reconnoitered ahead of cross-country fighting lumns that pushed ever outward from the airheads, dropped supplies, and ith the innovative STOL L-1's and helicopters) evacuated wounded. At the he, gliders were still unproven in Europe and Ike was less than comfortable th the idea of relying on an armada of them. Early word of their satisfactory rformance for Wingate assured a major role in OVERLORD.

Oddly, the Airborne control measures common in Europe were largely nored by Wingate. He refused to use any parachute troops, because he t their elitist mien made them unsuitable for molding into his patented in-ntion, the "Chindit."

Despite shortcomings, the Air Commando enterprise expanded the Air-rne concept by showing that a significant ground combat force pursuing strategic plan could be sustained solely by air. The "what-ifs" of applying e Air Commando approach to Airborne operations in other climes are con-derable. Even in the same area, the nearly-martyred Marauders could

have used their own Air Commando assets. Though allotted some in the last, desperate stages of taking Myitkyina, their suffering could have been miti-gated by more, earlier. As Cochran's band did not technologically represent much that was not in existence years before, what might have even a single composite squadron done for the 1942-1943 Airborne operations across north-west Africa? A handful of Wacos could have brought jeeps forward — even to places without airstrips — for the 509th, while "eye in the sky" duty by dedicated light planes might have helped keep tabs on the elusive enemy. Even in the more intense environment of the ETO, what if Brereton's Allied Airborne Army had acquired its own Air Commando Group in time for MARKET-GARDEN? Forward-based aircraft were not betrayed by the weather that cursed the troop carriers in England. They might have helped in many ways, even if only by flying in radios to the tragically silent British 1st Airborne Di-vision.

NOEMFOOR: IS THIS TRIP NECESSARY?

In early July 1944, the leapfrog campaign across the upper edge of New Guinea saw the separate 503rd Parachute Infantry Regiment make two battalion-sized jumps. Ostensibly these were combat assaults and necessary adjuncts to the amphibious landing on Noemfoor Island. As the 158th RCT waded ashore on 2 July, a Japanese prisoner confessed that 3,000 to 5,000 of his countrymen were laying low in the surrounding jungle, just waiting for the word to snuff out the American salient. This story reminded many of what had happened earlier at Biak; they vowed a recurrence would be averted. Word flashed to the on-call reserve force: the 503rd. With the dawn, the 1st Battalion chuted up at Hollandia and jumped in, fully expecting real combat.

The fact that the prisoner was mistaken aside, the drop proved to be an embarrassment. The airstrip called Kamiri that was the DZ consisted of tamped down crushed coral, every bit as unyielding as concrete. Construction engineers were busily at work there, not knowing or believing that the heroic skysoldiers were on the way to rescue them. There were dozens of bulldozers and like machines spotted about, working hard to make the hard surface harder yet.

Equipment lay-out for a commo man, February 1943, Gordon Vale, Queensland. In addition to the "walkie-talkie" short-range radio, signalling devices are the flares at left (carried in pouches meant for Thompson mags) and colored oilcloth marker panels (top center). (U.S. Army)

Thanks to his trusty machete, SSgt. Jones W. Gay of the 503rd PIR's 1st Battalion headquarters quaffs a cool one, jungle style. Port Moresby, New Guinea December 1943. (U.S. Army)

96

After its first combat jump at Nadzab, the 503rd PIR was augmented to become a self-supporting Regimental Combat Team (RCT) by the attachment of the 462nd Parachute Field Artillery battalion and Company C (only) of the 161st Engineer Battalion. The Engineers were later redesignated as the separate 161st Parachute Engineer Company. Here gunners of Battery C ply their trade at Camp Cable, outside Brisbane, 28 April 1944. Left to right: Francis J. Lorey, Steve Pruni, Joseph F. Kumiega and Henry H. Powell.

Medics of the 503rd display some supplemental rations at Port Moresby, 17 November 1943. Left to right: John Prendergast, Jelmer Blastad, and William Esquibel. The locally-fabricated pouches hold bandages and medical supplies.

In one of the Air Corps' miscalculations, the first planes came in at only 00 feet, the rest only slightly higher. The result: numerous injuries to the late jumpers.

On the 4th of July, the 3rd Battalion followed. With the constructors' behemoths pulled back and tucked in under the palm trees and the remorseful troop carrier crews minding their manners, the rate of injuries was lower. But the runways still broke bodies. Of 1,418 paratroopers deposited in the two lifts, 144 were busted up enough to be unfit for combat.

Despite the seemingly pointless casualties, some experts regarded this operation as a good one. It put otherwise idle paratroopers and fliers to work at their specialties for the first time since the Nadzab drop!

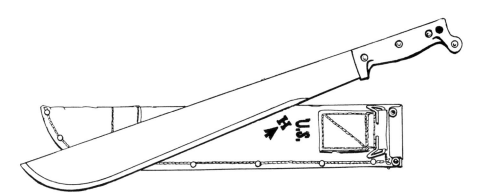

Several types of machete had been bought off-the-shelf for U.S. units, often as part of tool kits, before the adoption of a standard model. The 1939 pattern with 24-inch blade and leather scabbard was followed by the 18-inch model in web canvas sheath in 1942. Even in the ETO, they were in evidence — issued as on-board equipment for vehicles and to weapons crews for clearing fields of fire and cutting foliage for camouflage.

Mending the broken body of Sgt. Arnold Riewe is medic James Morris. The M-3 trench knife appended to the machete scabbard was typical 503rd practice. An M-2 jack-knife, blade stuck into the ground, is handy.

Company B, 503rd goes ashore at San Jose, Mindoro, on 15 December 1944. The first two men are dressed as "legs," but the third wears jump boots.

Pvt. Jack Paul, 501st Para Bn., prior to joining the 503rd enroute to the Rock. (QSI)

A paratrooper of Company G, 503rd blasts Japs on Corregidor with his bazooka. Note the folding M-1 carbine slung over his back. (CSM Lewis Brown)

HE ROCK REDEEMED: CORREGIDOR

Corregidor is an eminently fortifiable island that dominates Manilla Bay. 898, Admiral Dewey eased past its guns under cover of night. In the grim s of spring 1942, "The Rock" was the last bastion against the Japanese iressors. With great valor and suffering, its complement held out until over-elmed on 5 May. Douglas MacArthur kept faith with the martyrs. Though ct military necessity did not dictate that it be invaded and occupied, he a blood debt was due (and few expressed contrary views). Corregidor uld be taken — and the Airborne would lead the way.

On 3 February 1945, the non-divisional 503rd RCT was tagged for the The 11th Airborne Division was otherwise busy, and Col. George Jones' fit was not. Subsequent to mopping-up combat on Noemfoor and garrison y on Leyte, the RCT had been fighting on Mindoro. A parachute drop had n planned for Mindoro, but lack of space for staging an Airborne troop ier force on Leyte made an amphibious entry the only way to travel.

The ROCK Force consisted of the 503rd RCT and the 3/34th Infantry Regi-nt detached from the 24th Infantry Division. Planning was meticulous and ost nothing was unknown about the target. The island, a bit more than e miles long and half that across at its widest point, was shaped like a oole with a bulbous head and curved tail. The head was the highest ter-, a rough plateau with cliffs dropping over 500 feet to the sea. Here on pside" were the old garrison's headquarters and barracks — and the pa-e ground and golf course that would perforce serve as DZ's. At the waist, lowest area (called "Bottomside") would be the objective of the 3/34th's ohibious assault.

But intelligence had miscalculated the number of enemy personnel badly. inst an estimate of "600, mostly sailors," there were in fact a bit more 1 5,000 — most of them formidable Imperial Marines. Working for the at-ers was the Japanese commander's dismissal of warnings to prepare an Airborne landing. He had no idea that such a thing was possible. The likely DZ he could see was the old, overgrown airstrip far down the tail which was well-covered by his guns and a long way from anything impor-. The first unit to jump on the morning of 16 February was the 3/503rd forced with engineers and artillery), led by Lt. Col. John Erickson. Its mis-was to get in, hold on to the DZ's, and render support to the little beach-d.

The drop would be "thrilling": prevailing high winds dictated that the troop iers fly over two abreast, whizzing 600 feet above Topside for just six sec-s — long enough for perhaps eight paratroopers to bail out. It was reck-d that each jumper would drift something like 250 feet to the left in the rse of his 25-second descent, and that — if no human errors or wind shifts oped up — not too many would wind up over the cliffs into the drink or oped down in the enemy fighting positions that ringed Topside or hung n the precipice's foliage. In practice, the first sticks fell short and slammed d into rubble and shattered trees downslope of the target. Accuracy im-ved over the next hour and forty-five minutes of the first drop. To minimize altitude was cut to 400 to 500 feet with just six jumpers out on a circuit, casualties still ran a full quarter of the force.

Touch-down on "The Rock" — under conditions not taught at Fort Benning. Older white canopies are here mixed in with newer camouflaged ones and solid-colored cargo chutes.

The enemy command post fell quickly to vertical envelopment, its defend-ers having scant moments to shoot a few paratroopers before they died. With their leadership gone, no coordinated counterattack ever came. The 3rd Bat-talion took over the buildings and began working outward to get the measure of the problem, wiping out any opponents they found. They had ringside seats for the beach event — and PT boats running in to pick up sodden paratroop-ers. The Imperial Marines held their fire at first, then blazed away at the 3/34th from their cave positions in the face of the cliff beneath the Airborne.

The second echelon — the 2/503rd combat team under Maj. Lawson Cas-key — had fewer problems in the drop, but some Japanese had figured out the situation by then and fire was heavier. As they got to work rooting out concealed positions that threatened the DZ's and the beach, Col. Jones (present since the first drops) called off the third jump scheduled for the morn-ing. Losses were so much LESS than predicted, he felt secure in bringing in 1/503rd over the beach. The commander of the 1st Battalion interpreted this to mean there was no opposition — and had the C-47's drop his heavy

weapons and extra ammo on Topside because he wouldn't need it! Wh
they sloshed ashore the next afternoon, the folly of this was revealed.

On the nights of 17-18 February, Japanese Marines emerged to mou
banzai charges — up steep slopes, into the muzzles of the dug-in 3/34
The Airborne's turn came on the morning of the 19th. As the paratroope
shaved and prepared breakfast, more than 500 Nipponese berserkers pour
out of tunnel adits covered by rubble. One platoon was overrun before t
American response blossomed. Even then, action was fast and furious, w
many Airborne soldiers using bayonets, gunbutts, entrenching tools, and n
chetes for lack of time to reload. So many enemy bodies piled up that pa
troopers had to raise their knees and even feet to continue firing over the

The climactic cataclysm came the night of the 20th. Below the waist
the island rose Malinta Hill. Inside its mass was a series of large tunnels t
had been the command center of MacArthur and Wainwright back in 19
With bombardment-induced landslides sealing them in, the remaining Impe
al Marines had decided to go out in a blaze of glory. Once they had alm
cleared a passage to the outside, they planned to blow the last debris
with a small part of the tons of explosives stored in the tunnels. But the sche
literally backfired, causing an eruption so great that flame gushed out b
ends of the main tunnel to light up the sky. The upheaval killed six infant
men, and 600-odd surviving Japanese dazedly ran for the tail of Corregid
These and more were to perish later — 150 in a repeat of the big blast, play
out underfoot at Monkey Point. Americans killed three numbered 52. By
February, the last of the holdouts were done for. Japanese dead amount
to 4,500 confirmed and hundreds more atomized, while 455 G.I.'s had be
lost in action.

Gen. MacArthur's triumphal return to Corregidor came on 2 March, w
the 503rd turned out for the ceremonies. A week thereafter, the RCT sa
back to Mindoro and was alerted for another combat jump. This assist to
40th Infantry Division's landings on Negros Island was cancelled when
sistance proved weak, and once again the unit waded ashore for light inf
try service. Hunting down stragglers continued until the end of hostilities, a
processing thousands of surrendering Japanese then became the task. Thou
the colors of the 503rd PIR were not officially retired until they were States
on Christmas Eve, most of its soldiers had by then been sent home for
charge or transferred to the 11th Airborne Division.

**Another terrain appreciation of Corregidor. The soldiers at right wearing leggi
are from the 34th Infantry Regiment, 24th Infantry Division, that made a cc
dinated amphibious landing.**

**As the "Topside" field was covered liberally by Japanese fire, the rough ar
off the planned DZ became an acceptable alternative. (U.S. Army)**

This design was created to commemorate the Corregidor operation. It was not used as a pocket patch but rather as a shoulder sleeve insignia.

The 462nd PFAB's unauthorized emblem was used as both a jacket patch and as a decal applied to the sides of helmet liners.

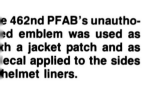

Wearing general purpose ammo bags as packs, a pair of paras survey the waterborne landings under way below. (U.S. Army)

As targets for spoil-sport snipers, and with no targets worth engaging, gunners of the 462nd PFAB stay low and mark time. The object in front of their piece is the breech block assembly of another howitzer. (U.S. Army)

ANGELS OF THE PACIFIC: THE 11TH AIRBORNE DIVISION

America's third major Airborne unit was activated at Camp Mackall on 25 February 1943. As fitting for the Airborne Division that would be most remote from the mainstream of Airborne warfare — and least impressed with the Airborne mystique and glamor — the day was not special. Only a small cadre was actually present for duty. The only units composed of volunteers — the 511th Parachute Infantry Regiment and its partner 457th Parachute Field Artillery Battalion — were at Camp Toccoa in the wild hills of northeastern Georgia. The 511th had been activated there the previous November. The artillerymen had been organized at Fort Bragg two months later, then migrated southward for jump school.

The 11th was the first Airborne Division to be formed in the fashion of most of the conventional units raised during the war — from the ground up, relying largely on levies of fresh draftees, OCS graduates, and faceless replacements. Very few of these men, even the parachute volunteers, were "masters of their own fate" or had sought such assignment. Even the cadremen were passed along from slightly more senior outfits, namely the 76th and 88th Infantry divisions. As herds of bewildered new guys arrived by train at all hours, they were grouped into units, had the news broken to them just what their occupational specialties were to be, and, by the way, that they were now in the Airborne! To their credit, they survived a difficult birth and coalesced into a capable outfit.

After basic and specialty training at Mackall, The Angels "saved the Airborne concept" through their performance in the "Knollwood Maneuvers" of 4-12 December 1943. These were inspired by bickering at the highest levels of the Army over the future of Airborne units. One faction — led by Chief of Army Ground Forces Gen. Lesley McNair — ballyhooed that flaws highlighted in Sicily were chronic and there was no place in upcoming invasions for Airborne units larger than regiments. The other faction was championed by the commander of the Sicily-battered 82nd Airborne, Matt Ridgway. Army Chief of Staff George Marshall answered Eisenhower's pleas for resolution of the argument by directing his man who had investigated the Sicily problems (Joe Swing, the boss of the 11th) to head an objective panel to conduct a test to decide the fate of the Airborne Division. This nine-day affair pitted The Angels against defenders played by the 517th RCT of the 17th Airborne Division. Under the scrutiny of the "Swing Board," McNair, and a host of dignitaries, the 11th made a huge success of it.

Thereafter, the 11th moved to Camp Polk, Louisiana, for its final maneuvers. While there, the policy of Maj. Gen. Swing that every one of his soldier should voluntarily qualify as a paratrooper resulted in the first divisional jum school at DeRidder Army Airfield. In April the 11th headed overseas and i late May arrived at Dobodura, New Guinea. There, training — including ar other jump school, plus glider, jungle, Alamo Scout, and endless amphibiou courses — occupied its attentions until it was pegged to follow up Dougla MacArthur's Return, the invasion of Leyte.

127th Airborne Engineers, Camp Mackall: Fred Brooks and pal with demolition bags. Brooks was nearly killed when chasing Japanese paratroops during their raid on San Pablo, Pearl Harbor Day 1944. Hit in the face and chest with many grenade fragments, his buddies assumed from his very bloody appearance that he was a goner and moved on. He was found, barely alive, by the medics and evacuated to a long convalescence. Attending his first reunion in 1989, some of his old comrades insisted that the man claiming to be Fred Brooks was an imposter, because they had seen him killed in action. (Fred Brooks)

On 18 November — as the Airborne troopers of the ETO halfway around e globe settled into rest camps between their Holland and Bulge battles The Angels entered combat for the first time. Landing at Bito Beach, The gels were assigned the task of pressing into the rugged tropical interior Leyte to break the back of Yamashita's forces.

From the 11th's baptism of fire, the gap between its parachute units and e rest of the Division began to widen. The main burden of the Leyte Moun ns mission was laid on the 511th paratroopers, while the 187th and 188th R's were left to secure the rear. Under Col. Orin "Hardrock" Haugen, the 1th RCT pushed slowly into the thick jungles and steepening mountain trails. panese resistance was fierce. Supplies were carried forward — and cas lties rearward — by hand. By 4 December, the 511th had taken the village Manarawat, sited on a rocky height surrounded on three sides by cliffs. forward command post for the Division was set up there, and a parachute uttle onto the tiny hilltop begun.

The commander of the 457th PFAB, Lt. Col. Nicholas Stadtheer, longed r gainful employment for his gunners, so he made a deal with the pilot of one air-sea rescue C-47 based back at San Pablo. In a series of 13 sorties, attery A and its guns (and later Battery D) jumped in to Manarawat. The 1th's own artillery spotter planes were also pressed into service, unloading ngle jumpers and dropping priority parabundles as needed. In this manner, ompany B of the 187th GLIDER Infantry, a platoon of engineers, and a non visional, non-previously-parachute surgical team were delivered. Seriously ounded men were flown out by the spotters from a minimal airstrip.

Though Leyte itself was to MacArthur a mere waystation en route to Luzon, e Japanese thought it a strategic thorn and hatched a grand plot to pluck . As part of an all-out counterattack, Tokyo directed the employment of its wn Airborne, the Raiding Group. Elements of the Parachute Brigade, with s 700-man 3rd and 4th Parachute Regiments, were sent against Tacloban nd Dulag on the coast, beginning with ill-fated parachute forays on 29 Novem er. A week later, the Katori Shimpei Force (a small battalion) was to jump n the Burauen area, to destroy aircraft, supply dumps, and parts of the 11th irborne Division. On the evening of 6 December 1944, over 40 Mitsubishi Sally" bombers and similar "Topsy" transports carrying about 300 jumpers it San Pablo — as Joe Swing spectated from the door of his command post.

As anti-aircraft fire rattled away, and the sons of the Emperor began to ake their presence around the base known with grenades and small arms re, the incredulous 11th troopers were quick to respond. Men of the 127th irborne Engineers and sundry headquarters personnel grabbed their gear — if not their pants — and ran or crawled from their tents. In a surrealistic ableau, American squads engaged furtive figures as they flitted through the oliage. For their moment of glory, the Japanese had fortified themselves with drug-laced liquor, and shrieked odd slogans like "All is resistless! Surrender es or no!" giddily tossing grenades and satchel charges through the night.

At dawn, with the 674th GFAB fresh on the scene, Gen. Swing led an old-fashioned charge. For several days afterward, the last of the Japanese paras — and larger groups of ground troops that had infiltrated — were hunted down, with the 1st Battalion of the 187th GIR and some "leg" infantry taking over the chase. Of the 51 Nipponese troop carriers dispatched from the

Making ready for the Tagaytay Ridge jump. Mae Wests were issued in case of splashes in picturesque Lake Taal. (U.S. Army)

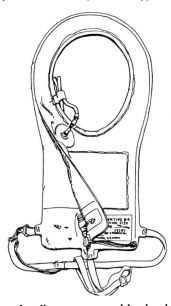

The B-4 life preserver of yellow-orange rubberized fabric — commonly known as the "Mae West," after a well-endowed Hollywood comedic actress — was an aviators' accessory passed on to Airborne. It was worn under the parachute harness, hence not as readily useful as drowning troopers liked.

Alamo Scouts: Team Nellist (minus two WIA) upon its return from the Cabanatuan prisoner camp raid, February 1945. Despite popular mythology, the Alamo Scouts were not a "unit," let alone an "airborne unit" — only six of the Alamo Scouts were paratroopers, three each from the 11th Airborne Division and the 503rd RCT. On 28 November 1943, the Alamo Scout Training Center was established under the auspices of the G-2, Sixth Army (codenamed ALAMO). It had the mission of training men from all services and even Allies. Of 500 graduates, most returned to their units, but some stayed at the Center in temporary-duty status. For specific operations, teams were selected from the Center. Through 1944, nearly all sorties — made by submarine, PT boat, seaplane, and rubber boat — were to check out potential airfields and beachheads for island-hopping invasions. They were also deliberately surreptitious — in and out, without the Japanese even noticing. One of the 10 teams involved in more than 60 forays was Team Nellist, which participated in the Cabanatuan raid on 30 January 1945, in coordination with Team Rounsaville (coincidentally also led by a jumper from the 11th), the 6th Ranger Battalion and Filipino guerrillas. The Filipino-American 1st Special Recon Battalion (earlier the 5317th Provisional Unit) and its supporting 978th Signal Company often provided linguist-guides and radio operators for Alamo Scout undertakings. (William E. Nellist)

Commo man Wil Moran avails himself of native transport on the Cavite road

airbase at Lipa on Luzon, 18 fell victim to ground fire, but at least nine dropped their loads at San Pablo and another 20 made it to nearby Buri. In the 11th' sector, the suicide squads got about a dozen light planes, as well as some supply dumps and vehicles.

Meanwhile, back in the jungle, rations became very short. Despite this the 511th PIR and the 2/187th continued the attack westward over the Ma honag Mountains toward Ormoc Bay. At Rock Hill, Lt. Col. Edward Lahti' 3/511th — which had been the paratroopers' vanguard since Bito Beach — pre vailed in a frontal attack up a steep ridgeline so narrow that platoons advance in column. For three days and nights, the battalion held on against infiltrator and head-on banzai charges. As this hill and the neighboring Hacksaw Ridg proved to be a main base of the enemy, seizing them was not enough. For two weeks, the 3rd Battalion and 2/511 under Lt. Col. Frank Holcombe beat of fanatical counterattacks. The tenacious Japanese were not broken until the 2/511, with the 2/187 in support, played turnabout, with a Yankee banza

...sion jump school, Lipa, May 1945. Once the 11th Airborne Division was out ...e battlelines, it set to work rebuilding and converting to the new tables of ...nization. In addition to absorbing replacements, it had to double its para-...per population quickly. The AIRBORNE tab sewn on the herringbone twill ...ue cap was de rigueur with the 11th by 1945, though the parachute disc seen ... was less prevalent. (U.S. Army)

The first style of herringbone twill (HBT) fatigues consisted of a jacket with waistband and trousers with inside-hung pockets. Replacing the blue denim work clothes beginning in 1941, these were at first justified as needed for the Armored Force — woolens quickly got irreparably stained around mechanized equipment. The following year, they became standard wear in the Southwest Pacific battle areas — and the later HBT shirt and trousers with large cargo pockets entered service. By 1945, the two styles had become the entire Army's hot-weather uniform.

The HB "mechanics cap" was another item conceived as part of the Armored Force work clothes wardrobe that spread throughout the service.

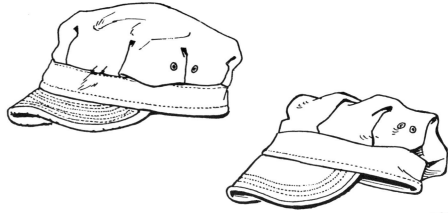

The "Joe Swing Hat" was an affectation of the 11th Airborne Division, especially during its Occupation days in Japan. Though similar to the issue HBT cap (and a civilian railroad engineer's cap), it was fashioned by tailors out of wool and khaki shirting, with exaggerated visor and top. It was worn with Class B shirtsleeve dress and even Class A with blouse.

Sixth Army commanding general Walter Kreuger drops by the Lipa airbase to wish well to the 511th before dawn, 23 June 1945. (U.S. Army)

A glider-landed gunjeep serves as headquarters for Brig. Gen. Pierson, overse of the Aparri operation. (U.S. Army)

on the night of 21-22 December. Then the 511th began expanding the link-up first eked out near Ormoc on 17 December. When the 511th was relieved for recuperation on Christmas Day, the 1/187 and 2/188 took over mopping up duties.

There remained an enemy hedgehog position halfway back to Burauen, at Anonang. Before the 11th Airborne Division could be entirely relieved, this had to be liquidated. After careful reconnaissance determined that there simply was no weak spot in the Japanese fortifications, it was decided that on 26 December the 1/187 would fake pulling out, then turn around and sneak back. Via a watered gorge, the return trip for the para-glidermen had them climbing the slopes of a rocky gully — hand over hand, by means of roots, vines, and outcroppings — to "flank," while the 2/188 and the Redlegs on Manarawat worked to keep enemy heads down. In two days and nights of ferocious combat, the dogfaces rooted the foe out of bunkers and spiderholes, in what came to be known as the Battle of Purple Heart Hill. This savage fight came days after Gen. MacArthur had publicized the end of all resistance on Leyte!

106

The 11th was reunited for a rest in January, but it didn't last long. (the 9th, landings on Luzon began at Lingayen Gulf, and a second front nor of Manila was opened on the 29th. The Angels were scheduled to condu parachute and glider insertions in support of these, but 5th Air Force balke professing lack of aircraft and preparation time. As an afterthought, the 11 was given its own, very narrow front south of Manila.

On 31 January, the majority of the Division went ashore at Nasugbu, pre-war beach resort 45 miles southwest of Manila. As the glider regimer brushed off opposition and rolled up the highway, the 511th was back on M doro, ready to jump wherever necessary. On the first two days of Februa the 188th GIR got entangled in a bitter engagement at Mount Cariliao, o side of the Aga Pass. The paratroopers were notified to jump on Tagayt Ridge early on 3 February.

As there were only some 50 C-47's available, the 511th RCT w transported in three lifts. The DZ was marked by ground-bound Pathfinde who crept forward with smokepots — and by the Division's G-3, circli in a liaison plane and decorating the place with white phosporous ha

TRAC's of the 672nd regain the friendly shore of Laguna De Bay, loaded with erated prisoners from Los Banos.

GYPSY Task Force links up: Angels of Company A, 511th PIR pleased to make the acquaintance of tankers supporting the advance of the 37th Infantry Division, Cagayan Valley, 26 June 1945. Only the officer at left is visibly an Airborne soldier — he wears jump boots. (U.S. Army)

nades. The first serial's drop of 375 men went fine, but then somebody confused and prematurely kicked out two door bundles. Notwithstanding pleas of aircraft crew chiefs, the next 540 eager paratroopers dove out and five miles short of the objective.

Given the dearth of enemy opposition on the DZ's, this would not have en so bad — but the noontime follow-up mission disregarded all signals, d dumped another 900 troops where they could see derelict chutes litter- the jungle! As a result, only about half of the 511th PIR joined in the fight t forced the Pass. The third and last airlift deposited the 457th PFAB on DZ, and it did contribute.

In the ensuing advance into Manila — into fiery rubble, roadblocks, barbed e, cratered streets, pillboxes, bunkers, anti-aircraft and large-caliber naval is in direct fire mode, plus aerial bombs and depth charges rigged as mines the 511th led the way, storming across the Paranaque bridge, into the Genko e, and up the runways of Nichols Field. The glider infantrymen spread out oss the rest of Nichols Field and onto Mabato Point, while Haugen's jump- hammered Fort McKinley and environs. Haugen himself died, one of 900 ualties in the Division (of which over 600 were in the glider infantry units) ore the capital was secured on 21 February.

The 11th Airborne will never forget losing out on the honor of being the laimed Liberators of Manila. The 1st Cavalry Division — larger and more ivily equipped — pierced the city limits from the north some six hours before Angels. Ironically, the Japanese had expected the main attack to come n the south and had weighted their defenses there; thus the heaviest Ameri- force faced the lightest defenses, and the lightest force the heaviest.

A scant two days after Manila fell, troopers of the 11th wrote a new and isual chapter in the Airborne legend. On 23 February 1945, The Angels de that monicker theirs forever in a raid on the internment camp at Los nos.

Mindful of the infamous Bataan death march and numerous reports of Japanese atrocities against prisoners and the Filipino people at large, MacArthur's HQ was sensitive to the plight of thousands of American and Filipino prisoners. As the liberators' frontlines approached well-known prison camps, steps were taken to make raids deep into enemy territory for the express purpose of saving the lives of captives. Following successful operations by the 6th Ranger Battalion and the 1st Cavalry Division, Gen. Swing had been alerted for such a job on 4 February, but got it postponed until the situation allowed him to disengage a unit for the purpose. The delay allowed his intelligence and operations staffs to achieve superior results.

South of Manila and east of Tagaytay, on the lower edge of the Laguna De Bay lake and more than 20 miles inside Japanese lines, Los Banos had thus far escaped attack. The camp was a former agricultural school, in which thousands of Americans and other foreigners — missionaries and military dependents among them — had been incarcerated and almost starved since 1942. The Filipino underground reported the camp had a guard force 247 strong and was secured by barbed wire fences, lookout towers, and pillboxes. There were an estimated 6,000 other enemy troops nearby and the Japanese had given no sign of any intention but stiff resistance. As the Japanese had an established reputation for savagery against the defenseless, and guards

at the Santo Tomas University camp had vowed to massacre 275 hostag[es] when the Cavalry had made that job part of their overt advance, it seem[ed] paramount to conduct the mission with all possible surprise. The Angels' G[-2] got the key tidbit of information from a recent escapee: at 0700 hours eve[ry] morning the guards fell in for PT.

The plan had several phases. First was the infiltration of the 11th's P[ro]visional Reconnaissance Platoon and 80 guerrillas by native canoes. T[he] force would lie in wait to secure a part of the lakeshore and a DZ adjoini[ng] the camp, then eliminate sentries at the appointed moment. Second, 51[1's] comamnder Col. Lahti (promoted upon "Hardrock" Haugen's death) pick[ed] Company B to accomplish the parachute phase. 1st Lt. John Ringler and [his] troopers were pulled from the line with little notice and trucked to s[till] smoldering Nichols Field.

Soon after briefings brought home to the combat-weary G.I.'s the spec[ial] nature of their mission, they drew chutes directly from planes that had brou[ght] up a shipment from New Guinea. Then they got ammo, checked their ge[ar] and curled up on the runways to catch up on their sleep. Nine C-47's hi[red] for the trip took off before dawn. At precisely 0700, Ringler spotted two smo[ke] grenades on the DZ and hit the silk at 500 feet altitude.

At the sight of the first canopy, Recon leader Lt. George Skau tappe[d a] bazookaman and a rocket streaked into the pillbox at the camp entran[ce.] A mere minute later the 155 troopers of Company B (reinforced by a mach[ine] gun platoon) were on the ground, and all guardposts under fire. Inside [the] camp, internees fell to the ground, thinking the Japanese were shooting [at] them. The calisthenics session dissolved as the Emperor's soldiers desp[er]ately scrambled for weapons. It took the raiders just 15 minutes to cover [the] 800 yards from the DZ (sandwiched between a railway and a high-volta[ge] powerline!), destroy three machine gun nests, put the torch to the guar[d] barracks, and kill 243 guards (at least 4 more were unaccounted for — in[ce]nerated or run off). Thereupon, they turned to the tearful task of getting [the] enfeebled internees ready to depart.

Paratroopers of the 511th march to waiting planes, Okinawa, 30 August 1945. Not knowing what sor[t of] "reception" the dastardly Japanese had in mind, the 11th at first tried to arrange a combat jump by a le[ad]ing battalion. But the B-24 bombers that had the range could not be adapted readily as troop-lifters, [so] higher-ups vowed that it wouldn't be needed. Thus, the 11th travelled light but combat-loaded, with tro[op]ers ready to fight to secure the Atsugi airfield. If men could not hump it, it did not go in the first da[y; note the laundry bags full of canned rations. (Col. Edward H. Lahti)

Troopers of the 188th PIR board a C-54 for the journey to Tokyo. (U.S. Army)

Just 40 minutes after landing, the raiders linked up with the third phase he raid. The remainder of Maj. Henry Burgess' 1/511th (with C/127th En- ers and half of D/457th PFAB) and their hosts, the 672nd Amphibian Trac- (Amtrac) Battalion, had made a dicey, night compass crossing of the lake won a minor shoot-out at the beach. With thousands more enemies nearby, e was not a minute to lose in loading up. But those freed were quite de- us with joy. The politesse of the paras was stretched thin in convincing m to hurry (encouraged by the burning of the camp huts and sounds of g), abandon their pitiful-but-cherished baggage, and get into the bizarre, x-like LTV's. The 2,136 internees were so underweight nearly all of them ld be packed into the 59 "Buffalos" in a single lift. The second lift took the rest of the captives and all the raiders.

The fourth phase of the classic raid was the diversionary attack down the d between Manila and Los Banos. The 1/188th GIR, 675th GFAB, and attached 472nd FAB, rounded out with a company of tank destroyers, struck at 0700, drawing the attention of enemy tactical units in the area. e the withdrawal across the lake was accomplished, this force fell back, ping possession of only a newly won bridgehead and high ground on the side.

Until late April, the 11th had no time to rest on its laurels. It kept going ugh southern Luzon, fighting as light infantry. When V-E Day came, The els were just moving in to their new rest camp at Lipa. There, another p school and other retraining schemes held sway, until the Airborne was t needed.

On 23 June 1945, the major part of the 511th RCT — embodied as GYPSY k Force — conducted a parachute-glider landing near Appari, a small sea- t on the northern coast of Luzon. For the first time in the Pacific, gliders some C-46 drop ships were used. Six CG-4A's and one of the new, larger -13's carried artillery. The concept of the operation was to deny the port apanese remnants and catch them between the Airborne and oncoming und columns.

But the rapid advance of the latter turned the move into a mere reinforce- t by air. The only combat came when the paratroopers attached them- es to the heavy forces for patrols and sweeps of suspected enemy ngholds.

Back at Lipa, training intensified. Okinawa, China, and mainland Japan ored objectives. Using the time to convert to the new, bigger and better orne Division tables of organization, Gen. Swing redoubled his efforts ualify all his men as parachutists. He also went so far as to unilaterally esignate the 188th GIR and its associated 674th GFAB as Parachute units! was NOT what Washington had intended.

Rather, the 541st PIR — lately Airborne Command's demonstration unit, ce highly proficient — was dispatched overseas for the expressed pur- e of becoming the second PIR of the 11th Airborne Division. When Col. at McEntee arrived with his regimental advance party on 10 July, he was ly informed that his unit was out of business and his soldiers would be ged into units throughout the 11th. It took a month for the Pentagon to e up the struggle but the inactivation of the 541st was made official on August 1945.

Here the regimental commander models the warm weather dress that prevailed in the 511th: Col. Lahti at Tomioka navy barracks, Yokohama, early September 1945. (Col. Edward H. Lahti)

When the first A-bomb devastated Hiroshima, The Angels were still at Lipa. But when the second mushroom cloud made capitulation likely, the 11th began air movement to Okinawa for the purpose of staging for landing in Japan. As C-47's did not have long enough legs for the journey, C-46's and B-24 bombers were used. Six crashed, taking some 60 paratroopers to their eternal reward. After two weeks of austere camping out in puptents, alternating between heat

Col. Lahti visits Hanamkai-Onsen to see the 1st Battalion, October 1945. Maj. Lawson B. Caskey, formerly of the 503rd RCT, sports the wool version of the modish "Joe Swing hat" and casual shirt collars, while the boss pairs the new field jacket (adorned with an all-embroidered 511th "oval" with wings) with officers-only dark olive shirt and trousers. (Col. Edward H. Lahti)

and dust and typhoon downpours, the first-arrived 511th RCT was alerted for a combat drop. Test jumps were made from B-24's, with poor results. No matter: higher headquarters decreed that the Japanese were really trustworthy, hence combat preparations were out! The Airborne soldiers were, however, skeptical about the wonderful folks who had brought the world Pearl Harbor.

The final scheme centered on a fleet of four-engined Douglas C-54's. These were by no means tactical airlifters and not compatible with paradrops. For eight days, they flew shuttles on the 1,600-mile leg, bringing forward the rest of the 11th, plus an assortment of detachments, the press corps, cargo, and jeeps. After a two-day weather hold, the largest, furthest airlanding yet began, at 0100 hours on 30 August. At Atsugi, Swing and his retinue debarked. He brushed off the reception committee's polite welcome, and demanded their samurai swords, forthwith. The 511th had been bumped (from first to last), and the honor of being the first unit in passed to the green 3/188th — followed by assets the Division staff thought essential: the honor guard and band.

In the afternoon, Gen. MacArthur was greeted and escorted into Yokohama. As the motorcade passed, Japanese soldiers lining the route did about-face and bowed their heads to show their great disgrace in defeat.

The Angels moved in for Occupation duty amongst the ruins. For the first weeks, the 511th got the port city of Yokohama. Their neighbors were the 4th Marine Regiment, which coincidentally had "Airborne in its blood." The pre-war 4th Marines had been lost in the fall of the Philippines in 1942, but when the Marine Parachute Regiment had been inactivated to provide cadre to new "leg" units, the two units had been consolidated to merge histories. The 188th took possession of the Fujisawa area, while the 187th fell heir to Atsugi. The rough and ready Airborne troopers were confounded by culture shock. They had never suspected the Japanese people of being civilized or rational or having any redeeming traits at all.

On the 15 September, the 11th began redeployment to northern Honshu. Most of the Division moved to Sendai, while the 511th was remoted to Morioka. Through the autumn, the troopers settled into their new homes and undertook patrols to show the flag and enforce the military government edicts that were remaking every aspect of Japanese life. As the "Home by Christmas" drive to discharge high-point vets took hold, personnel from the inactivating 503rd RCT showed up to take their places. Many new men (volunteers for the Regular Army obligated for long hitches) came from non-Airborne units, so a fourth jump school was convened. By then, the 11th's bailiwick had been extended to include the isle of Hokkaido; a slice of the Division base and the 187th assumed the burden. As units were pulled in to fewer caserns with better facilities, the grip of the Peacetime Army tightened — even families settled in. But for even the unmarried, the lot of the conqueror was splendid. The good duty was almost too good to be true, with training and parades and sports balanced by geishas and booze and tourism.

In May 1949, the 11th was shipped home, with Fort Campbell, Kentucky its new base. In the context of Japan, this was to cut costs of the Occupation and demonstrate the faith the United States had in the progress of Nipponese democracy. It was also inspired by a wish to lessen tensions with the Soviets and the new Communist regime in China — who found a capital Airborne Division worrisome — and a feeling that a second worldwide contingency force had a place back home. Thirteen months later, the onset of the Korean War made it seem an Airborne force of some size should have been kept in the Far East!

These "Para-Glider wings" were created overseas (without War Department authorization) by troops of the 11th Airborne Division, to reflect graduation from both jump school and the glider qualification course.

EEPING THE HOME FIRES BURNING: AIRBORNE COMMAND

The Airborne Command supervised the Airborne effort Stateside. It was sponsible for generating succeeding waves of combat-ready Airborne units well as development of new methods and materiel. It was heir to the Provisional Parachute Group, created 10 March 1941, the quasi-regimental headquarters for the separate Parachute Battalions and the infant parachute training course at Fort Benning. The wide-ranging reorganization of the Army after Pearl Harbor brought the expansion of subordinate units to Parachute Infantry Regiments, and so the assets of the Group were used to form a higher echelon Airborne Command on 23 March 1942.

The Command's work to activate, man, train, equip, and prepare units for overseas deployment was a Herculean task, but its parallel efforts to develop better equipment and techniques in coordination with the USAAF and the many branches of the Army were no small projects either. As Fort Benning, the Home of the Infantry, could no longer nurture all things Infantry and support the many units being activated there, in April 1942 the "ABC" moved to Fort Bragg, North Carolina.

Bragg had originally been a field artillery post, large enough for big guns to fire freely from one end to the other. As it already had a major tenant in the 9th Infantry Division (until it left for Tunisia), the "ABC" had to make do with available facilities. The 503rd PIR was its first progeny, with one of its battalions (later famed as the independent 509th Battalion) dispatched to England in June and the remainder sent to Australia in October. Soon the Airborne presence at Bragg outstripped all others: both the 82nd and 101st Airborne Divisions arrived, to rendezvous with their PIR's and begin the training cycle that would qualify them for overseas. Though the 9th was leaving, the need for more troop cantonments, maneuver areas, airstrips, and facilities for the Airborne led to the establishment of an outlying base in the so-called Sandhills Recreation Area.

This was operational under the title "Camp Hoffman" (after the nearest town) from February 1943, but once the "ABC" had transferred its flag there, it was officially named for the first paratrooper killed in action, Pvt. Tommy Mackall. The new cradle of the Airborne became legendary, as a "garden spot." Its tarpaper-clad, ultra-austere temporary buildings — for up to 32,000 troops — sprawled across gritty pine barrens. It was said that winter winds indoors equalled the icy blast of a parachute jump, strong enough to blow the helmet off a soldier's head. Five movie theaters and six beer gardens helped morale enough to avert insurrection.

Mackall was not enough. With the activation of the 11th and 17th Airborne Divisions, it teemed with four divisions and sundry other units. To provide training with aircraft, non-divisional units (under the 1st Airborne Brigade) were sent to the Troop Carrier base in Alliance, Nebraska, in April 1943. When the departure of the "All American" allowed, the 2nd Airborne Brigade was activated in July, followed by the 13th Airborne Division in August.

As units moved overseas and passed from its control, the Airborne Command had less and less to do. While its testing and Parachute School duties remained constant, it otherwise was fated to work itself out of a job. reorganized as the less grand Airborne Center on 1 March 1944 (but still

ABC surgeon Maj. Marshal Brucer shows his latest badge: glider QUALIFICATION wings, 7 March 1944, Camp Mackall. The Airborne Command and Airborne Divisions then Stateside began awarding these for completion for a training course. Meanwhile, in Europe the 82nd and 101st first awarded the glider badge for PARTICIPATION in the combat landings in Normandy. (John C. Grady)

111

the "ABC"), it focused on familiarization training for customers outside Airborne realm. This included combined air-ground training with Troop rier aircrews and glider pilots, demonstrations for interested parties such the Command and General Staff School and the Air Forces School of App Tactics, and air-transportability courses for six standard infantry divisic Other contributions to the war effort were a liaison detachment with the F Airborne Army and, through two "road show" units, star billing in the 1 War Bond drives.

Chief among the Command's long-term units were the 541st and 54 PIR's, the 555th Parachute Infantry Battalion, the 467th PFAB, and the 59 Parachute Engineer Company. The 541st was stripped of men to provide placements after Normandy, Holland, and The Bulge, then rebuilt and s to the Philippines. The 542nd was reduced to a Battalion on 17 March 19 In an ironic twist, its members were discouraged from volunteering for c bat — demonstrators had higher priority! When inactivated on 1 July 19 its assets were recast as the ABC Training Detachment: one infantry c pany, an artillery battery, a special troops company and a headquarters. V the discontinuation of ABC in December 1945, the Detachment moved to F Benning to become part of The Parachute School, itself thereafter (and o again) subordinate to the Infantry Center.

"HOOK UP!" A vivid memory — the jumpmaster's bellow commands the stick to click their snap hooks to the anchor cable. (John C. Grady)

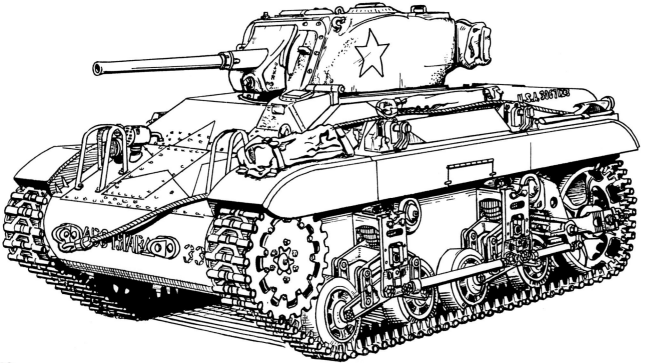

The T-9E1/M-22 "Locust" Airborne light ta was never employed overseas by Americ forces, but the British landed a few in Han car gliders in VARSITY. It was the project the Marmon-Herrington firm, begun late 1941 on the assumption that the Fairch C-82 and Laister-Kaufman CG-10 aircr would be available to carry it. Even as sm as it was (eight short tons empty), it was t heavy for true Airborne operations. It was a mechanically unreliable and undergunned. total of 1,900 were ordered, but only 830 a tually built.

gt. Paul Huff, who won the Medal of Honor while serving with the ▌th PIB in Italy, finished the war with the Airborne Command. This ▌ture, taken in 1945, points up the fact that the M1942 jump suit con-▌ued to be THE paratrooper uniform back in the States long after it ▌ been superseded overseas. Note that the Technician 3rd Grade ▌dic combines the special aidman's pouch with ordinary web gear. ▌ron Holl via the 542nd Parachute Infantry Association)

The first Fairchild C-82 Packet made available to ABC. The promising "Flying Boxcar" project began in 1941, but the firm's lack of experience with large, complex aircraft delayed fruition of the first American purpose-built airlifter. If it had been ready as predicted in early 1944, fully-assembled howitzers, 1½ ton trucks, and even M-22 light tanks might have been dropped in OVERLORD and later operations. (John C. Grady)

The hard way to move a howitzer around: five human draft animals of the 467th PFAB pull and five helpers push to get a pack 75 off the DZ. At 1,296 pounds, the section can only be hoping the terrain gets better soon.

The Army parachutist qualification badge with "R" added for "Rigger

A WAC with jump wings! Pvt. Marie McMillen, a rigger with credentials as a world-class sport parachutist, does a "Women at War" broadcast from Fort Benning, July 1944. The possibility that she is actually on jump status and officially recognized as a military parachutist is reinforced by the fact that she wears the background trimming of The Parachute School behind her wings (that bear a block-letter "R") and the parachute cap disc. (U.S. Army)

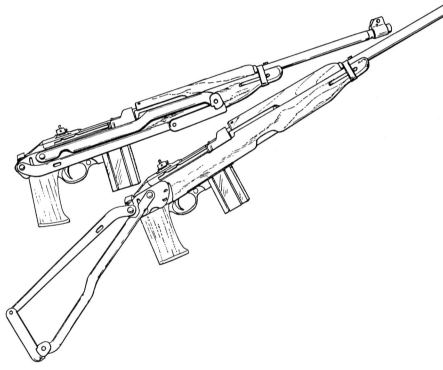

A sight to bring tears to the eyes of an old jumper: the control tower at Camp Mackall. (542nd Parachute Infantry Association)

In actual service, the hastily conceived M-1A1 folding-stock carbine proved u comfortable to fire and incapable of surviving the shock of launching grenade The M-1A2 used a sliding stock much like that of the M-3 SMG, but with a so buttplate — which proved too fragile for sustained grenade work. The M-1A design — mating the larger rear grip of the A2 with a stronger pantographic sto made of sheet metal — was standardized for mass production, but Airborne Co mand withdrew its requirement because Airborne troops were by then jumpi with full-stock carbines or foregoing them for rifles and submachine guns.

Other units of the "ABC" were the 407th Field Artillery Group and 215th and 465th GFAB's, which left the Airborne prior to overseas service; and elements once intended to be organic to the never-activated 15th Airborne Division — the 515th PIR, 410th Airborne Quartermaster Company and 715th Airborne Ordnance Company. The 515th ultimately went to the 13th Airborne Division and Europe, while the 410th and 715th were "deconverted" from Airborne and sent to the Pacific.

Though not formed by the ABC, there were other Airborne units. The 151st Airborne Tank Company and 28th Airborne Tank Battalion were born at Fort Knox to operate the M-22 "Locust." The Anti-aircraft Artillery Command built an airlanding force equipped with .50 caliber machine guns amounting to six battalions and 59 batteries (all of the former and 45 of the latter seeing combat, notably in the Mediterranean and CBI). Of three battalions of lightened 40mm guns created, one fought at Myitkyina, Burma. Seven of 12 Airborne Engineer Aviation Battalions entered battle — three each in New Guinea and Europe, one in the CBI. While the tank outfits were expected to land by glider, the others were Airborne only in the sense of their capability to be packed into tactical transports for follow-up landings inside airheads; none had Parachute sub-units.

In late 1944, the Airborne Command dispatched a liaison team to Europe to investigate enemy and Allied Airborne-related materiel and to advise the First Airborne Army staff. Men of ABC/ETO here include Lt. Paul Duncan (center) and rigger SSgts. Wilmer Willett (top) and Stan Harrison (sitting). (John C. Grady)

The 1st Parachute (later Airborne) Infantry Brigade was subordinate to the Airborne Command and wore that shoulder patch (approved 22 March 1943) until inactivated in January 1944. The 2nd Airborne Infantry Brigade may not have worn its emblem approved 4 August 1944, as its HQ was by then attached to HQ, 82nd Airborne Division. Jacket patches in ABC included those of the 541st PIR, the 542nd PIR/PIB, and the Airborne Training Detachment.

TRIPLE NICKEL: DESTINY FORECLOSED

The only Negro paratroop unit, the 555th Parachute Infantry, came of age only after the possibility of its going overseas had passed. Formed as an independent Company on 30 December 1943, the unit was upgraded to the 555th Parachute Infantry Battalion on 25 November 1944. The Battalion struggled to prove itself — as a fighting outfit to be taken seriously, comprised of soldiers every inch the equal of white paratroopers — against the smothering "Jim Crow" system of degradation and double standards.

When first embodied, the Triple Nickel's home was Ft. Benning. There, where the "Colored" 24th Infantry Regiment of the Regular Army had long been active, and paratroopers had already cut a wide swath through cafe society. Black paratroopers moved with relative ease in an established (though segregated) community. When transferred to Camp Mackall, this changed. In North Carolina, racism raged unchecked, on and off post. Adversaries — even inside the Airborne Command itself — helped ensure that The Nickel did not easily qualify for overseas duty. The biggest stumblingblock was manpower. Despite (some say because of) the demonstrated high quality of its men, the lifeblood of new volunteers was kept to a trickle. Men worthy of commissions in non-Airborne units stayed sergeants, while many high school graduates stayed PFC's. In the face of seething frustration, morale was helped by strong discipline and emphasis on pride. Personal appearance and military bearing were unsurpassed.

In 1945, the 555th drew a consolation prize: a peculiar secret mission in the Pacific Northwest, called "Operation Firefly." It was suddenly important for the Army to run a flying fire department!

Smokejumpers were needed to counter the hush-hush threat of Japanese fire balloons. This peril was serious, serious enough to be kept from the public until after the war, as only lack of word on results caused Tokyo to cancel the project. Between November 1944 and May 1945, over 9,000 "Fu-Go" balloons were launched from Honshu, loaded with five- and ten-pound incendiaries and 32-pound fragmentation bombs. More than 200 of these were "hits" that caused forest fires or other damage, including the deaths of unwary civilians. Hundreds more made it to America, but were derelict "misses" strewn from Alaska to Mexico, defeated by the strong winds and deep snowdrifts of winter.

Tim Garrett of the 555th PIB poses in the door, outfitted in field-expedient smoke-jumper gear that is a mixture of military issue and civilian types. As the Forest Service coveralls were in short supply (none had been made since the war began, and most were from 1939 or earlier), riggers took USAAF sheepskin flight clothing and modified it, with crotch-saving stirrup webbing and big canvas collars. Riddell football helmets were shipped out from Fort Benning and given faceshields. His boots are civilian loggers' types.

Through the especially bad fire season of 1945, the "Black Panthers" the 555th reacted from staging bases at Chico, California, and Pendleton, regon. From their first for-real jump on 14 July, they reinforced white Forest ervice firefighters (many of them Conscientious Objectors doing alternative ervice) in 36 fire-suppression jobs involving over 1,200 individual jumps. Each vent meant four to six days on the ground "in the middle of nowhere," working to exhaustion, and humping out equipment to the nearest road for pickup. ivilian and military techniques intermixed — C-47's had greater payload and nge than the best foresters' plane, a Ford Tri-Motor. To troopers, the steerole chutes, tools, padded jump suits, and Geological Survey maps were weird. Vhen not being scorched, they recovered downed balloons and stray ordiance, and assisted the civil authorities. The racial attitudes of local folks aried from virulent hatred to refreshing hospitality, averaging out to differnt non-fraternization.

In September 1945 — the war over — the main body of the Battalion reurned to North Carolina, and attachment to the 13th Airborne Division. Despite an infusion of new volunteers, the turbulence of demobilization, endless abor details, and neglect from on high kept the unit in the doldrums — until

the advance party of the 82nd showed up. The arrival of Maj. Gen. Gavin changed everything. He thought bigotry was stupid, counter-productive, and had no place in the Army. Backed by combat veterans familiar with the performance of Black G.I.'s in battle, and the gradual gaining of the upper hand within the Army by non-racists, he put an end to the long dry spell. The 555th took part in the New York Victory parade and others, becoming a showpiece. Strength peaked at 1,309 paratroopers in November 1946, provisionally aligned as a bob-tailed quasi-regiment.

Gavin launched his own integration program. Athletic teams and honor guards were opened to all and training merged; recreation, family services and housing were improved; in December 1947 he inactivated the 555th and transferred its men to the 3rd Battalion of the 505th PIR, the 80th Airborne AAA Battalion, and individual slots throughout the "All American." Seven months later, President Truman (with an eye on the upcoming election) finally issued the order proclaiming "equal treatment and opportunity" for all in the military; even it did not end segregated units.

117

Paratroopers of the Triple Nickel en route to a fire jump, Pendleton, Oregon. From left: Stout, Jackson, Hanks, Crosby, Wildrose, Lt. Lane (standing), unknown, Hargrove, Groom, Rivet, Ware, Waters, and Reeves; on the floor, Thrasher and ''Tex.'' (Carl Reeves)

The full ensemble of smokejumper apparel as used by the U.S. Department of Agriculture Forest Service in 1945. The coverall is of heavy brown duck, with red patches on the shoulders and cuffs (to facilitate spotting jumpers from the air). Unlike military parachutists, smokejumpers were taught that landing in a tree was better than chancing coming down on who-knows-what on the surface. Consequently, they aimed themselves for cross-branches and spread their legs for impact — the stout webbing strap that ran inside the coveralls from the hips, under the feet, and just below the crotch averted disaster. The stirrup section of that webbing, and the quick-release tabs that made getting in and out of the suit easier, can be seen. Once safely arrived and hanging in a friendly tree, the smokejumper sat on branches, tugged his canopy off the foliage, attached the chute harness to the tree, and shinnied down the shroud lines. If he was still far-removed from solid ground, the reserve chute was next, followed by the 50 feet of rope carried in the large pocket on the lower leg. (U.S. Department of Agriculture)

NORTHERN BROTHERS: CANADIAN PARATROOPERS

Canada had considered forming Airborne units as early as November 1940, but not until the British 1st Airborne Division was a going concern were steps taken to incorporate the Canadian Parachute Corps. In July 1942, a call for volunteers was issued and on 1 August a battalion was authorized.

To expedite matters, the first Canadian paras were sent to the United States for parachute training. The first 28 graduated at Fort Benning on 11 September. Over the next six months, at least 100 others followed, and some stayed on to learn the nuts and bolts of Airborne training. In the same period, more volunteers from units in Britain began passing through the jump school run by the RAF, and 85 of them returned to Canada. By March 1943, the Canadian Parachute Training Centre was fully operational, at Shiloh, Manitoba.

At Shiloh, the Benning Influence was strong. Not only were American training procedures adopted, but parachutes, jump kit and aircraft as well. Even the uniform was affected, by the addition of Corcoran-type jump boots (made in Canada) to both training and walking-out dress. Later, when the 1st Battalion served with the British 6th Airborne Division (from 28 July 1943), its peculiar dress distinctions of bloused jump boots and wings worn on the chest were a source of irritation to their British fellows.

Maj. Routh of Canada's first class of paratroopers receives American jump wings from the commandant of The Parachute School at Fort Benning, November 1942. Routh later commanded the Canadian parachute school, but missed out on the war in Europe. Instead, he served in the PACIFIC with U.S. units, as a supernumerary liaison officer tasked to learn the American way prior to the use of Canadian troops there (planned, but not realized). As such, he made the Noemfoor jump with the 503rd before moving on to duty in India and Burma with the "Chindits." His badges are those of his old unit, the Royal Rifles of Canada — his prewar Militia battalion that perished in the defense of Hong Kong and subsequent "Death March."

The cap badge of the CPC was made in "bi-metal" (silver and gold) and brown plastic (often painted gold). Only officers wearing Service Dress had need for the bi-metal collar badges.

Once the initial cadre was trained, the Canadian Parachute School was set up at Shiloh, Manitoba. Here a stick emplanes on a Lockheed Ventura of the school's organic flight. All their gear — except for Sten guns and chevrons, is American issue acquired through Lend-Lease. (Col. Randall Routh)

The color "Rifle Green" was selected for the first shoulder title (and background of the jump wings) of the Canadian Airborne because its senior officers were seconded from Rifle units. The second title, worn overseas, retained the green as a border while taking up the maroon of the British.

Canadian jump wings were worn on the left chest, something not allowed their British counterparts. The Canadian Parachute Corps encompassed the 1st "Can Para" that joined the British 6th Airborne Division, the Canadian contingent of the 1st Special Service Force that was administratively designated the 2nd Battalion CPC by Ottawa, and the depot at Shilo, Manitoba.

Our quest for previously unpublished photographs related to the history of American Airborne forces has by no means ended. We continue to seek pictures, documents (including orders and reports of all types) and other materials for future use. Veterans of Parachute, Glider, Troop Carrier, Special Forces, Ranger, and OSS service having personal snapshots, military publicity or newspaper photos, or "lost" official prints generated at unit levels that would be suitable for publication are encouraged to contact the publisher. With your help, the story of the "unsung" can be published.

Rear cover photographs:

Leslie L. Rich, Jr., 509th PIB, Le Muy, 15 August 1944; Pvt. Ernie Ernstein, MP Platoon, 101st Airborne Division, Bastogne, 27 December 1944; Maj. Gen. James M. Gavin, 82nd Airborne Division, Berlin, September 1945; Pvt. Eugene Tamgelder, 188th Parachute Infantry Regiment, Yokohama, September 1945.

WE WISH TO ESPECIALLY THANK:

Tony Accristo	Paul S. Frye	Elmer Noll
John Alicki	Turner Fuss	George Petersen
Robert Anderson	Ets Galassi	Ken W. Powers
Bob Baldwin	Emery Graham	Earl Price
David Berry	John C. Grady	Dr. Charles Pugh
Dr. John Brunner	Charles T. Graul	Dick Reardon
CSM Lewis Brown	Gene Harvey	Carl Reeve
Fred Canziani	O.B. Hill	Jack Risler
Col. Frank Clagett	Walter Hughes	George Rosie
William Colby	Lee Hulett	Bill Ryan
Doug Bailey	William Knarr	Jack Paul
Tony DeMayo	Richard Lacefield	LTG Richard Seitz
Bill DeSalvo	Col. Edward H. Lahti	Gordon Smith
John Despot	Carl Leydig	Bill Story
Robert Durkee	Jake McNiece	Herb Schumacher
Dr. John Duval	George Morris	Charles Snyder
Roger Tallakson	Kenneth Tucker	Col. C. Young
Jim Welsh	Gerald Yonetz	LTG Wm. P. Yarborough
Charles Fairlamb	R.W. Koch	

CHRONOLOGY
U.S. AIRBORNE IN WORLD WAR II

39

May — War Department memo to Chief of Infantry asks for study of air landed troops. Reply downplays concept of units landed in powered aircraft, suggests parachute delivery.

40

Apr — War Department approves proposal for a parachute test unit at Fort Benning, Georgia — to be implemented as soon as aircraft and parachutes can be obtained.

May — HQ US Marine Corps investigates parachute units.

Jun — Call for volunteers from the 29th Infantry Regiment for the Parachute Test Platoon, Fort Benning, Georgia.

Jul — PTP travels to Hightstown, New Jersey, to try out jump towers.

Aug — First parachute jumps by PTP. Battle cry "Geronimo!" originated.

Aug — Fifth and last jumps made by Parachute Test Platoon.

Sep — Army constitutes "1st Parachute Battalion"; designation amended to "501st," 2 Oct.

Oct — USMC Commandant directs battalion of each infantry regiment to be "Air Troops," with one parachute and three airlanding companies.

Oct — 501st Parachute Battalion activated at Fort Benning.

Oct — First class of 40 Marines begins parachute training at Lakehurst Naval Air Station, New Jersey.

Nov — Most of privates in 501st designated "parachutist specialist" to qualify for extra pay; flight pay had been given to PTP members.

Dec — First "Prop Blast Ceremony," at Fort Benning.

6 Dec — Final qualifying jump for first "Paramarines" at Lakehurst.

1941

21 Jan — Office of the Quartermaster General proposes a qualification badge for Army Parachutists designed by Captain William P. Yarborough.

26 Feb — Combined graduation of first and second Marine parachute troops at Lakehurst; former also qualified as riggers.

10 Mar — Provisional Parachute Group organized at Fort Benning. Design for Parachutist wings approved, made by Bailey, Banks & Biddle, Philadelphia, Pennsylvania.

22 Mar — First ceremony for award of Parachutist Badge, Infantry School commandant BG Omar Bradley presiding.

28 May — First USMC parachute unit, Company A, 1st Parachute Battalion, activated at Quantico, Virginia.

28 Jun — Company C, 501st Parachute Battalion leaves Fort Benning for service in Panama.

1 Jul — 502nd Parachute Battalion at Fort Benning, and 550th Infantry Airborne Battalion at Fort Kobbe, Panama Canal Zone, activated.

10 Jul — The Parachute School at Fort Benning authorized.

15 Aug — USMC 1st Parachute Battalion activated at Quantico.

28 Aug — USAAF authorizes 150 officer aviators to qualify as glider pilots.

1 Oct — USMC 2nd Parachute Battalion activated, Camp Pendleton, California.

10 Oct	88th Infantry Airborne Battalion activated at Fort Benning.

1942

10 Jan	USMC Glider Detachment formed at Parris Island, South Carolina; expanded to Glider Group MGL-71 on 24 Apr.
19 Feb	USAAF implements plan for 1,000 glider pilots — aimed at volunteers from within the Army, including enlisted men and washouts from powered-aircraft flight schools.
23 Mar	Airborne Command activated, with units and TPS subordinate.
14 May	Waco delivers first XCG-4; 640 CG-4A ordered off the drawing board.
6 Jun	2nd Battalion, 503rd PIR dispatched to Britain.
7 Jun	Marine 1st Parachute Battalion leaves Norfolk for Pacific Theater.
10 Jun	USAAF authorizes recruitment of glider pilot trainees with no previous flight experience, including civilians.
28 Jun	With only sport sailplanes in Army inventory, the first Glider Pilot wings are awarded at war bond airshow in Washington.
9 Jul	1st Special Service Force activated at Fort Harrison, Montana.
25 Jul	1st SSF begins parachute training.
20 Jul	1st Parachute Infantry Brigade activated, Fort Benning; designation changed to Airborne, 6 Apr 43. (Previously subordinate to 1st Division since 1917; returned to 1st Infantry Division in 1964.)
27 Jul	First Airborne anti-aircraft unit, 700th Coast Artillery Battery, activated and attached to 88th IAB.

7 Aug	First American parachute unit enters combat Marine 1st Parachute Battalion makes amphibio raid on Gavutu Island in support of Guadalcanal vasion.
15 Aug	First two US Army Airborne Divisions created at Can Claiborne, Louisiana. Elements of already-active 82 Infantry Division (motorized) reorganized as Glid with some transferred to newly-activated 101st. P achute units transferred in and formed new.
4 Sep	"Wings Parade" for 1,200 men of 1st SSF.
15 Sep	OSS Detachment 101 formed in India.
16 Sep	USMC 3rd Parachute Battalion activated.
22 Oct	503rd PIR (-2nd Battalion, then in England) depa for Australia, en route picks up 1/501st in Panan
28 Oct	Marine 2nd Parachute Battalion attacks Choiseul land; fighting withdrawal via PT boats of LT John Kennedy.
8 Nov	First U.S. combat jump; 2/509th PIR, Algeria, O| ration TORCH.
15 Nov	2nd Bn, 509th PIR drops at Youks les Bains, Alger
21 Nov	Flight Officer rank authorized for Glider Pilots.
6 Dec	31 men of 2/509th PIR Scout Company (and t French soldiers) jump at El Djem, Tunisia; efforts interdict enemy lines of communications fail; 24 s vivors exfiltrate.

1943

7 Feb	First operational jump by OSS — recon team of (U.S. & Burmese), Detachment 101.
10 Feb	505th PIR assigned to 82nd Airborne Division, repl ing 326th GIR and reversing glider/parachute rat
25 Feb	11th Airborne Division activated at Camp Mackal

Mar	Camp Mackall, North Carolina, formally dedicated; named for Pvt. John T. Mackall, 2/509th PIR, first Army paratrooper killed in action (died of wounds inflicted by Vichy French aircraft, 12 Nov 42, in Algeria).
r	T-9E1 airborne light tank enters series production, which lasts until Feb 44.
Apr	Marine 1st Parachute Regiment activated. OSS 2677th Provisional Unit formed at Algiers from assets of "Experimental Detachment," AFHQ.
Apr	17th Airborne Division activated at Camp Mackall.
May	82nd Airborne begins disembarkation at Casablanca, Morocco.
May	First mass tactical glider landings with troops and equipment, in Carolina maneuvers.
May	USMC glider effort ended with disbandment of Marine Glider Group MLG-71 at Eagle Mountain Lake, Texas.
Jun	2nd Airborne Infantry Brigade activated at Camp Mackall.
ul	505th PIR and 3/504th PIR make combat jump at night near Gela, Sicily (HUSKY I). First combat for U.S. Glider Pilots; 30 volunteers in Wacos land British LADBROKE Force near Syracuse.
Jul	504th PIR (-3rd Bn) makes night jump (HUSKY II) near Gela; nervous reaction by US AAA downs 23 of 144 C-47's, with 318 casualties to paratroops and aircrewmen.
Jul	1st Special Service Force departs San Francisco for the Aleutians.
ug	Setback to Glider program with crash of CG-4A carrying mayor and dignitaries at St. Louis, Missouri; investigation highlights folly of numerous underqualified contractors.

11 Aug	151st Airborne Tank Company activated at Fort Knox, Kentucky.
13 Aug	13th Airborne Division activated at Fort Bragg.
16 Aug	Parachute drop by 2nd Regiment; 1st SSF on Kiska cancelled due to mysterious disappearance of enemy.
5 Sep	503rd PIR makes combat jump at Lae, New Guinea, reinforced by 31 Australian artillerymen; scheduled glider mission cancelled.
8 Sep	Operation GIANT II — a coup de main planned to take Rome with cooperation of Italian forces — aborted; planes carrying 504th RCT recalled in midflight. Meanwhile, unrecalled detachment of 509th and OSS land by boat on isle of Ventotene to knock out radar.
12 Sep	First parachute insertion of OSS Operational Group, at Decimomannu airfield, Sardinia.
13 Sep	504 PIR makes short-notice night jump into Salerno; first U.S. use of Pathfinders and EUREKA.
14 Sep	505th PIR follow-up jump into Salerno. 2/509th jumps into rough terrain around Avellino; scattered troops resort to guerrilla warfare, then exfiltrate.
6 Dec	Knollwood Maneuvers to prove viability of Airborne Divisions and large-scale night assaults begin in the Carolinas. 28th Airborne Tank Battalion activated at Fort Knox; reorganized as non-Airborne 20 Oct 44.
30 Dec	555th Parachute Infantry Company activated at Fort Benning.

1944

28 Feb	Airborne Command discontinued, replaced by Airborne Center. First glider combat mission for 5318th Provisional Unit in Burma.
29 Feb	At midnight, Marine 1st Parachute Regiment inactivated.

5 Mar	Operation THURSDAY, airborne invasion of Burma, begins.
14 Mar	Design for Glider wings approved.
20 Apr	Hazardous duty pay extended to Glider troops who are parachute-qualified; applied to all assigned Gliderman, 1 Jul 44.
23 May	2677th Provisional Unit reorganized as "OSS Regiment."
25 May	11th Airborne Division disembarks in New Guinea.
6 Jun	OVERLORD: 82nd and 101st Abn Divs make night-drop into Normandy.
28 Jun	OSS OG's begin jumps into Vercors area of southern France in support of upcoming Operation DRAGOON.
3 Jul	1/503rd PIR parachutes onto crowded airstrip at Noemfoor, New Guinea; 2/503rd follows next day.
15 Aug	DRAGOON: 1st Airborne Task Force lands in Southern France.
25 Aug	XVIII Corps (Airborne) established as higher HQ of ETO Airborne.
17 Sep	Operation MARKET-GARDEN, invasion of Holland begins.
13 Oct	Operation AZTEC — OSS OG parachutes into Venice area.
27 Nov	Operational Groups Command, OSS organized (Stateside).
4 Dec	Using borrowed air-sea rescue C-47 and Piper Cubs, Battery A, 457th PFAB, infantry and engineer detachments drop onto mountaintop of Manarawat, Leyte. First and only combat jump for elements of nominally-Glider 187th Infantry.
6 Dec	Japanese paratroops raid 11th Airborne Division rear area in San Pablo-Burauen, Leyte.
23 Dec	Parachute and glider resupply missions into Bastogne.

1945

31 Jan	11th Abn Div (-511th PIR) makes beach landings at Nasugbu, Luzon.
3 Feb	511th PIR jumps on Tagaytay Ridge, south of Mani
6 Feb	13th Airborne Division arrives in France.
23 Feb	Raid on Los Banos prison by 511th PIR and attachmen
22 Mar	Two Waco gliders used for emergency resupply Ramagen bridgehead; medical gear flown in, wound flown out.
24 Mar	Operation VARSITY Airborne assault at Wesel, G many. Operation RYPE: OSS Norwegian Special O Group (NORSO) jumps at Jaevsjo.
20 Apr	Gliders land engineer units and supplies at Lewa, I laywa, and tennant in Burma; leapfrog missions to z yatkwin, 5-8 May.
13 May	555th PIB moves to Pendleton, Oregon, to support C eration FIREFLY.
18 May	Epic rescue of survivors of C-47 crash in mounta of New Guinea begins with jump of two medics fr U.S.-Filipino 1st Recon Bn. Nine more paras and gli landing follow; all personnel flown out in gli snatches, 28 Jun-1 Jul.
23 Jun	Task Force GYPSY lands by parachute and glider Camalaniugan airstrip at the town of Aparri in nor ern Luzon.
27 Jul	Chinese 2nd Commando and OSS OG inserted parachute to raid Chaking River traffic in Operati BLUEBERRY.
15 Aug	Operation CARDINAL, OSS Mercy Team, jumps Mukden, Manchuria, to secure safe release of pris ers including Gen. Wainwright.
26 Aug	13th Airborne Division returns to Fort Bragg from E rope, to prepare for the invasion of Japan.
27 Aug	Chinese 3rd Commando and OSS OG jump into Na king (Operation CHERRY).
30 Aug	11th Airborne Division begins landing in Japan.

CHRONOLOGY OF ARMY GLIDER
AND PARACHUTE INFANTRY UNITS

7th	Constituted	12 Nov 42	Activated	25 Feb 43	
8th		12 Nov 42		25 Feb 43	
9th		26 Dec 42		13 Aug 43	Disbanded 8 Dec 43
0th		26 Dec 42		13 Aug 43	Disbanded 4 Dec 43
1st		18 Jan 43	not activated		Disbanded 4 Oct 51
2nd		18 Jan 43	not activated		Disbanded 4 Oct 51
3rd		16 Dec 42		15 Apr 43	Disbanded 1 Mar 45
4th		16 Dec 42		15 Apr 43	Inactivated 14 Sep 45
5th	Activated	25 Mar 42	Redes GIR	15 Aug 42	
6th	Activated	25 Mar 42	Redes GIR	6 Aug 42	Inactivated 25 Feb 46
7th	Activated	25 Feb 42	Redes GIR	15 Aug 42	Inactivated 30 Nov 45
1st	Activated	15 Aug 42	"3/325", "3/327" from early 44		Disbanded 1 Mar 45
1st	Constituted	24 Feb 42	Activated	15 Nov 42	Disbanded 20 Aug 45
2nd		24 Feb 42	Activated	2 Mar 42	Inactivated 30 Nov 45
3rd		24 Feb 42	Activated	2 Mar 42	Inactivated 24 Dec 45
4th		24 Feb 42	Activated	1 May 42	
5th		24 Jun 42	Activated	6 Jul 42	
6th		1 Jul 42	Activated	20 Jul 42	Inactivated 30 Nov 45
7th		24 Jun 42	Activated	20 Jul 42	Inactivated 16 Sep 45
8th		6 Oct 42	Activated	20 Oct 42	Inactivated 25 Nov 46
9th	(2nd Bn)	2 Nov 42	Activated	5 Oct 41	Redes 509th PI Bn 10 Dec 43
1th		12 Nov 42	Activated	5 Jan 43	
3th		26 Dec 42	Activated	11 Jan 43	Inactivated 14 Sep 45
5th		18 Jan 43	Activated	31 May 43	Inactivated 25 Feb 46
7th		16 Dec 42	Activated	15 Mar 43	Inactivated 25 Feb 46
1st		6 Aug 43	Activated	12 Aug 43	Disbanded 10 Aug 45
2nd	no record		Activated	1 Sep 43	Redes Bn 17 Mar 44 In 1 Jul 45
3rd		3 Sep 43	Not Activated		Disbanded 4 Oct 51
4th		3 Sep 43	Redes 545th	20 Sep 43	
5th		20 Sep 43	Not Activated		Disbanded 4 Oct 51
0th	(Bn only)	10 Jun 41	Activated	1 Jul 41	Inactivated 1 Mar 45
1st	(1st Bn)	30 Oct 42	Activated	26 Nov 42	Inactivated 10 Feb 45
5th	(Co)	25 Feb 43	Activated	30 Dec 43	Redes Co A, 555th PI Bn
5th	(Bn)	9 Nov 44	Activated	25 Nov 44	Inactivated 15 Dec 47

NOTES